ROBERT COLLIER'S

THE SECRET OF THE AGES

OTHER TITLES IN
THE **INFINITE SUCCESS** SERIES

Adam Smith's The Wealth of Nations

Benjamin Franklin's The Way to Wealth

Bertrand Russell's The Conquest of Happiness

Carl von Clausewitz's On War

Charles Mackay's Extraordinary Popular Delusions and the Madness of Crowds

Frank Bettger's How I Raised Myself from Failure to Success in Selling

Fred Schwed's Where are the Customers' Yachts?

George S. Clason's The Richest Man in Babylon

Karl Marx's Das Kapital

Miyamoto Musashi's The Book of Five Rings

Napoleon Hill's Think and Grow Rich

Niccolo Machiavelli's The Prince

Ralph Waldo Emerson's Self Reliance

Samuel Smiles' Self-Help

Sun Tzu's The Art of War

ROBERT COLLIER'S

THE SECRET OF THE AGES

A MODERN-DAY INTERPRETATION
OF A SELF-HELP CLASSIC
BY KAREN McCREADIE

Copyright © Infinite Ideas Limited, 2010

The right of Karen McCreadie to be identified as the author of this book has been asserted in accordance with the Copyright, Designs and Patents Act 1988.

First published in 2010 by
Infinite Ideas Limited
36 St Giles
Oxford, OX1 3LD
United Kingdom
www.infideas.com

All rights reserved. Except for the quotation of small passages for the purposes of criticism or review, no part of this publication may be reproduced, stored in a retrieval system or transmitted in any form or by any means, electronic, mechanical, photocopying, recording, scanning or otherwise, except under the terms of the Copyright, Designs and Patents Act 1988 or under the terms of a licence issued by the Copyright Licensing Agency Ltd, 90 Tottenham Court Road, London W1T 4LP, UK, without the permission in writing of the publisher. Requests to the publisher should be addressed to the Permissions Department, The Infinite Ideas Company Limited, 36 St Giles, Oxford OX1 3LD, UK, or faxed to +44 (0) 1865 514777.

A CIP catalogue record for this book is available from the British Library

ISBN 978-1-906821-38-8

Brand and product names are trademarks or registered trademarks of their respective owners.

Designed and typeset by Cylinder

BRILLIANT IDEAS

INTRODUCTION	8
1. FIND YOUR OWN TRUTH	10
2. WE ALL HAVE SUPERHUMAN ABILITIES	12
3. THE EVOLUTION OF KNOWLEDGE	14
4. THE CONSCIOUS AND SUBCONSCIOUS MIND	16
5. THE POWER OF INTUITION	18
6. THE PECULIAR CHARACTERISTIC OF THE SUBCONSCIOUS MIND	20
7. COLLECTIVE CONSCIOUSNESS	22
8. THE AMAZING ABILITIES OF MIND	24
9. YOUR SUBCONSCIOUS NEVER SLEEPS	26
10. WHAT IS PRAYER?	28
11. WE CAN DO ONLY WHAT WE THINK WE CAN DO	30
12. A LITTLE BIT OF PHYSICS	32
13. DON'T THINK OF ABRACADABRA	34
14. GARBAGE IN, GARBAGE OUT	36
15. UNUSED TALENT DECAYS	38
16. A FAIRY-WISHING RING	40
17. MENTAL BROWNIES	42
18. THE LAW OF VISUALISATION	44

19. IT'S THE LITTLE THINGS THAT COUNT	46
20. THE DANGER OF 'TRUTH'	48
21. IT'S WRITTEN ALL OVER YOUR FACE	50
22. TAKE THE PEBBLE OUT OF YOUR BOOT	52
23. THINKING VS ASSOCIATION	54
24. SEEK GROWTH – BUT AVOID THE GOLDEN HANDCUFFS	56
25. ON MARRIAGE	58
26. YOU DON'T NEED TO KNOW THE DETAIL	60
27. THE IMPORTANCE OF PERCEPTION	62
28. BE OPTIMISTIC	64
29. GOOD NEWS FOR COUCH POTATOES	66
30. THE LAW OF ATTRACTION	68
31. MAKE THE WORLD BETTER	70
32. KARMIC JUSTICE WILL PREVAIL	72
33. THE DISCOURAGEMENT DISEASE	74
34. THINGS YOU CAN CONTROL VS THE THINGS YOU CAN'T	76
35. FEAR IS CREATIVE THOUGHT IN NEGATIVE FORM	78
36. MIND OVER MATTER	80
37. FIRST MIND, THEN BODY	82
38. TO FEAR OR NOT TO FEAR, THAT IS THE QUESTION	84
39. UPS AND DOWNS OF LIFE	86
40. WIPE THE SLATE CLEAN	88
41. RELAX	90
42. LIFE WILL FIND A WAY	92
43. THOUGHT IS THE DIRECTION, EMOTION IS THE FUEL	94

44. THE TIME IS NOW	96
45. IT'S THE INVISIBLE THINGS THAT REALLY MATTER	98
46. ASSUME A VIRTUE	100
47. SPECIALIST VS GENERALIST	102
48. INITIATIVE	104
49. PRICELESS WISDOM OF BOOKS	106
50. AGE IS IRRELEVANT	108
51. THE MEDICINAL DELUSION	110
52. AND FINALLY... THE MINDBENDER	112
CONCLUSION	114
REFERENCE MATERIAL	116
INDEX	122

INTRODUCTION

When I was asked if I would like to write a modern interpretation of *The Secret of the Ages* by Robert Collier, I had to confess I'd never even heard of it. I had a vague familiarity with Collier, but only in so far as I'd seen his name attributed to various quotes in personal development books.

So I read his work and I became intrigued. I really loved the way he expressed some of the ideas and his thinking was very much in line with my own observations and experiences about the mind and its influence over our lives.

I was surprised to read two poems that were written in Napoleon Hill's classic, *Think and Grow Rich*. One of those poems might have been a coincidence but both of them made me quite certain that Hill had probably studied the work of Robert Collier. After all, Collier lived many years before Hill. In fact, *The Secret of the Ages* was published in 1926, some eleven years before Hills' contribution.

Theologian and author John of Salisbury first wrote about this evolution of ideas back in 1159, in a Latin treatise on logic called *Metalogicon*. Salisbury said, 'We are like dwarfs sitting on the shoulders of giants. We see more, and things that are more distant than they did, not because our sight is superior or because we are taller than they, but because they raise us up, and by their great stature add to ours.'

Perhaps mathematician and physicist Sir Isaac Newton had read that treatise because in 1676 he wrote a letter to his rival, natural philosopher Robert

Hooke. In it he wrote, 'What Descartes did was a good step. You have added much in several ways… If I have seen a little further it is by standing on the shoulders of giants.'

Newton stood on the shoulders of giants, as did Hill and most probably Collier himself. Great authors of this or any other subject would be foolish not to study the works of others so that they can add their thoughts and evolve that thinking into new areas of study and understanding. There can be little doubt from reading *The Secret of the Ages* that Collier, for example, also studied the works of William James, James Allen, Emile Coue and Wallace Wattles, to name but a few.

Collier himself is said to be one of America's original success thinkers and part of the New Thought movement. New Thought was a spiritual movement developed in the US during the late nineteenth century with an emphasis on positive thinking, law of attraction, healing, personal power and creative visualisation. Pioneering psychologist and philosopher William James referred to New Thought collectively as a 'Mind-cure movement'. Following an undiagnosed illness, of which he later managed to cure himself, Collier became fascinated by the mind and set out to write a book on practical psychology. *The Secret of the Ages* was the result. Initially the chapters were split into separate books and within six months of publication, he had received over $1 million worth of orders, selling over 300,000 sets in all. Sadly I doubt this little companion will reach those lofty heights, but I hope you enjoy it nonetheless.

This is a modern look at what Collier originally wrote about, an attempt to see what others saw as they stood on his, and subsequent giants' shoulders. It is not a substitute for the original, but offers a unique insight into what has since been discovered and what questions those discoveries pose. Considering the financial woes of the world as I write this little book, perhaps it's about time that we appreciated the incredible value of the little bit of real estate we all have – the space between our ears!

1 FIND YOUR OWN TRUTH

Collier says, *'It matters not whether you believe that mankind dates back to the primitive ape-man 500,000 years ago, or sprang full-grown from the mind of the creator.'* I couldn't agree more, but sadly the world is still full of hate and intolerance based on these very different viewpoints.

DEFINING IDEA...
There is nothing either good or bad, but thinking makes it so.
– WILLIAM SHAKESPEARE

On one hand, scientific consensus states that 't = 0' – the beginning of the world – occurred some 13.7 billion years ago. What would become human beings first made their appearance a mere 5 million years ago. The more upright version that we recognise as man appeared well over a million years ago. According to Bill Bryson's best-selling book, *A Short History of Nearly Everything*, '... all of these evolutionary jostling over five million years... produced a creature that is still 98.4% genetically indistinguishable from the modern chimpanzee. There is more difference between a zebra and a horse.'

At the other extreme we have Creationism, a Christian fundamentalist movement that is usually based on a literal interpretation of Genesis: 1–2. In other words, the Earth is just a few thousand years old and God created everything in it over seven days. Creationists believe this to be true – not a metaphor, but an actual account of what happened.

Will we ever really know for sure which view is correct? Certainly, the evidence mounts for the first, yet there are millions of people who believe the latter. In the end, something is true when we believe it to be true.

Indeed, I encourage you to question everything and then work out if what someone is telling you is true for you. I have no problem with organised religion per se. If your faith fosters understanding and offers you comfort in times of trouble or helps you become a better person, then great. But if your religious beliefs foster hate and intolerance and fill you with guilt and shame, is that really helpful? Is it making your life better?

I was staggered to read samples of the hate mail received by Richard Dawkins, author of *The God Delusion*, and fellow questioners. In my view, we have the right to believe whatever we want to believe. If you believed that the power of thought was just some new age bullshit, then I would think you an idiot but I wouldn't want to 'take a knife, gut you fools, and scream with joy as your insides spill out in front of you' (sent to Brian Flemming, author, film-maker and atheist). I wouldn't, 'hope you get a painful disease like rectal cancer and die a slow, painful death' yet that was the message sent to the editor of *Freethought Today*. I don't remember those teachings in Sunday school!

Collier reminds us, 'in the beginning, this earth was just a fire mist – six thousand or six billions years ago – what does it matter which?' In truth, it doesn't. What does matter is that your beliefs influence your life, so why not choose beliefs that help and support you to be the best you can be?

HERE'S AN IDEA FOR YOU...

Thinking of the two views above, which do you believe to be true? What evidence do you have to support your theory? Have you just blindly accepted an opinion based on your parents' convictions or have you investigated it for yourself to work out what you believe? If you haven't done so already, perhaps it's about time you did.

2 WE ALL HAVE SUPERHUMAN ABILITIES

Collier talks of the 'Life Principle' within us all: *'It is the reserve strength of the athlete, the "second wind" of the runner, the power that, in moments of great stress or excitement you unconsciously call upon to do the deeds which you ever after look upon as superhuman.'*

DEFINING IDEA...
Where there is great love, there are always miracles.
~ WILLA CATHER, AUTHOR

In *Think and Grow Rich*, Napoleon Hill implies that this reserve strength occurs when we have a 'definite major purpose' and 'burning desire'. Similarly, in *The Secret of the Ages*, Collier tells the story of how two teenage boys lifted a huge log off their brother, who was caught underneath. The next day, four grown men could not lift the same log! It is fair to assume in that moment of panic those boys had only one 'definite major purpose' and a 'burning desire' to save their brother, but is it all just urban myth?

While some stories definitely are so, there are verifiable cases of extraordinary feats in the face of adversity. On 9 April 1982, Angela Cavallo's teenage son Tony was fixing his 1964 Chevy Impala when the jack slipped and pinned him underneath. He was knocked unconscious. Desperate to save her son, Angela – then in her late fifties – was able to lift the car off him for 5 minutes while a neighbour ran for help and someone else reinserted the jack. The boy made a full recovery.

Scientists Michio Ikai and Arthur H. Steinhaus demonstrated that human strength could be increased up to 31% by panic, certain pharmacological agents or hypnosis. In an article published in the *Journal of Applied Physiology* in 1961, they concluded that what we think we are capable of is based on 'Pavlovian procedures' – conditioned responses that come to inhibit our full potential. In other words, we are all capable of great feats that are far above what would be considered 'normal' but in reality, it takes a crisis for us to tap into that capacity.

Therein lies the rub. Most of us don't have a burning desire or definite major purpose to activate our inner strength and demand we step up to the plate. There is no catastrophe to focus our efforts, no last-chance saloon that demands we dig deep and access this inner power. Perhaps change is easier when everything sucks! If your relationship is OK, but not brilliant, if your job is OK, but not brilliant, if your life if OK, but not brilliant, then you are in limbo. It's too good to leave, but not good enough to stay. You want more, but at the same time feel guilty because, 'it's not *that* bad!'

Crisis seems to provide direct access to this power, but it's not the only way. Consciously taking charge of your thinking through disciplined focus and creative visualisation can also bring about the results you seek. Collier reminds us, however, that 'The greater your need, the more readily will it respond to your call.'

> HERE'S AN IDEA FOR YOU...
> *Take a few moments to think about your life as it is. What would you change? List three things you would like to change. Taking each one in turn, consider how important it is. Unless there is a burning desire to make the changes they will fall by the wayside like impotent New Year's resolutions. Genuine desire for change is the key.*

3 THE EVOLUTION OF KNOWLEDGE

In his book, Collier highlights the evolution of knowledge and how that has helped us grow and develop: *'From the lowly cave man, cowering in his burrow in fear of lightning or fire or water to the engineer of today, making servants of all the forces of Nature is but a measure of difference in mental development.'*

His words remind us how we instinctively fear what we don't understand. From the beginning of recorded time, great thinkers have been persecuted for going against accepted 'wisdom' – especially if those ideas fly in the face of religious doctrine.

DEFINING IDEA...
To announce truths is an infallible receipt for being persecuted.
~ VOLTAIRE, FRENCH WRITER AND PHILOSOPHER

In 1543, Polish astronomer and mathematician Nicolas Copernicus published a book that suggested that the Sun, not the Earth was the centre of the universe. This of course challenged the Church and went against what was written in the Bible. Copernicus' view was based on his observations of astronomy and his expanded knowledge of the way the world worked. He was correct, yet his work was placed on a list of forbidden books and not removed from that Index until 1835. Although he died of natural causes before the Church could get to him, others were not so lucky.

When scientist Giordano Bruno confirmed Copernicus' calculations and suggested the Sun and its planets may be one of many systems in an infinite universe he was accused of blasphemy. He was arrested in 1592 by a department of the Church called the Inquisition. Following a lengthy trial, Bruno was branded a heretic and burned at the stake in 1600. Galileo Galilei, another scientist who also supported Copernicus, was called before the Inquisition but because he was a personal friend of the Pope he got off lightly with house arrest until his death in 1642.

Galileo is often deemed the 'father of modern science' because he based his work on empirical observation and mathematics. But it wasn't a fairytale that he was telling – that was reserved for the other side of the argument!

It's not just the Church that is to blame, however: the scientists themselves made some major errors as knowledge evolved. In 1908, when amateur geologist Frank Bursley Taylor suggested the continents looked as if they were once connected, he was largely ignored, but Alfred Wegner, a German theorist and meteorologist, thought he was on to something. How else might we explain the fact that animal fossils of the same – or similar – species turned up on different sides of the planet? According to geologists of the time, the solution to this anomaly was to invent 'land bridges'. These creatures would have walked over land bridges to get to where they were going! Seriously, this was the accepted wisdom taught and considered 'truth' for over half a century despite not a shred of evidence in support of it – which of course there couldn't have been since it was complete fiction.

Collier reminds us of the need for an open mind, common sense and a willingness to test theory and search for evidence instead of blindly following the pack.

HERE'S AN IDEA FOR YOU...
Can you see the evolution of knowledge in your own life? Think of three things that you used to believe as true which you later worked out were false. How did you learn they were wrong? Usually we learn from new teachers, be that through books, visiting new cultures or enjoying new experiences.

4 THE CONSCIOUS AND SUBCONSCIOUS MIND

Collier says, *'The one most important province of your conscious mind is to center your thoughts on the things you want, and to shut the door on every suggestion of fear or worry or disease. If you once gain the ability to do that, nothing else is impossible to you.'*

DEFINING IDEA...
It is psychological law that whatever we desire to accomplish, we must impress upon the subjective or subconscious mind.
~ ORISON SWETT MARDEN, WRITER

Since Collier wrote his book there have been many theories about the conscious and subconscious mind and how each bit is made up. In 1967 neurologist Paul MacLean came up with an evolutionary model of the brain, known as the 'triune' brain. The oldest part of the brain is the reptilian brain, followed by the limbic system and finally, the neocortex (or rational) brain. Sigmund Freud muddied the waters in the 1920s when he suggested the subconscious was nothing more than an impulsive force in a constant tug of war with the more logical and detached conscious mind. Some view the two as part of the same system, while others such as Peter Dayan, a theoretical neuroscientist at University College London, together with fellow scientists Nathaniel Daw and Yael Niv, see the mind comprising of four systems.

There is also debate as to where the subconscious ends and the conscious mind begins. Studies carried out in the 1990s by Stanislas Dehaene, director of the Cognitive Neuroimaging Unit at INSERM, demonstrate we are aware of things that our conscious mind does not register. For the purposes of this book, however, it's probably not that important which is correct — we don't need to understand how electricity works before we can use it, do we?

The most helpful description I've ever found about what's really going on in your mind comes from Bruce H. Lipton's fantastic book *The Biology of Belief*, in which he states, 'The conscious mind is the creative one, the one that conjures up "positive thoughts". In contrast, the subconscious mind is a repository of stimulus-response tapes derived from instincts and learned experiences. The subconscious mind is strictly habitual; it will play the same behavioural responses to life's signals over and over again, much to our chagrin.'

Most probably you will have experienced this yourself when something trivial has sent you into a tailspin and you've later on been confused by your own over-reaction. Indeed, something just pushed your buttons and you reacted to a long-forgotten association that delivered a knee-jerk reaction. According to Lipton, 'When it comes to sheer neurological processing abilities, the subconscious is millions of times more powerful than the conscious mind.' So, if your conscious desires conflict with the programmes running in your subconscious mind, they will come to nothing.

Left to its own devices, the subconscious will run amok over your hopes and dreams. But if you understand the challenges you face and train your conscious mind to harness the power of the subconscious then anything is possible. Collier states, 'Our subconscious minds are vast magnets, with the power to draw from universal Mind unlimited knowledge, unlimited power and unlimited riches.'

HERE'S AN IDEA FOR YOU...

If you want to change, you must learn how to tap into the subconscious mind so that you can, where necessary, overwrite negative or unhelpful programming. This can be assisted by techniques such as Neuro Linguistic Programming (NLP) and hypnotherapy. Alternatively, just master your thoughts.

5 THE POWER OF INTUITION

Collier says the subconscious mind was, *'the only mind animals had before the evolution of the brain; and it could not, nor can it yet, reason inductively, but its power of deductive reasoning is perfect'*. There is therefore some other intelligence that trumps our conscious one every time!

DEFINING IDEA...

Thinking doesn't seem to help very much. The human brain is too high-powered to have many practical uses in this particular universe.
~ KURT VONNEGUT, NOVELIST

In his fascinating book *Blink*, Malcolm Gladwell explores this 'other' intelligence. He opens by telling the story of a marble statue – known as a 'kouros' – supposedly dating back to the sixth century BC. Back in September 1983, an art dealer offered it to the J. Paul Getty Museum in California for just under $10 million. Of the 200 known kouros in existence, most had been recovered badly damaged and yet this example was almost perfectly preserved. The museum curator was ecstatic, but cautious. He took the kouros on loan and began a thorough investigation. The paperwork was checked, high-resolution stereomicroscopes, electron microscopes, probes, mass spectrometry, X-ray diffraction and X-ray fluorescence were used to establish the age and authenticity of the statue. Tests proved the stone was indeed ancient.

And yet there were dissenting voices during the process. Among them was Evelyn Harrison – one of the world's foremost experts on Greek sculpture. When she was shown the statue in the Getty just before the deal was done, the then curator Arthur Houghton whisked off the cloth covering the work and with a flurry said, 'Well, it isn't ours yet, but it will be in a couple of weeks.' Harrison replied, 'I'm sorry to hear that.' To this day, Harrison doesn't know what she saw in that statue but instinct told her this was a fake. Other well informed people had the same reaction. When former director of the Metropolitan Museum of Art in New York Thomas Hovering saw the work, he immediately asked, 'Have you paid for this? If you have, try to get your money back. If you haven't, don't!'

Neither expert nor the host of others who agreed with them could tell the curator exactly how they knew the kouros wasn't right – they just knew. Fourteen months after the investigation began the Getty was satisfied and bought the kouros because the science said it was genuinely old. Subsequent investigations have shown the kouros' documentation was fake and experts still stand by their gut response. Even the Getty displays the kouros as, 'Greek, about 530 BC or modern forgery'.

This instinctive insight or inexplicable gut response is known as 'thin-slicing' and refers to the ability of our unconscious to find patterns in situations and behaviour based on a very narrow slice of experience. And it is hugely undervalued in the modern world. Ironically, US author and futurist John Naisbitt makes a really good point when he says, 'Intuition becomes increasingly valuable in the new information society precisely because there is so much data. Unless we learn to trust our first response we are in danger of suffering from increasingly bad cases of analysis paralysis.'

HERE'S AN IDEA FOR YOU...

When you meet someone for the first time, take note of your initial response and don't edit it or assess it. Learning to trust that initial gut response might be quicker and safer than any ID card or security system we could ever develop.

6 THE PECULIAR CHARACTERISTIC OF THE SUBCONSCIOUS MIND

Collier quotes from a Dr Pitzer, who apparently states that the subconscious mind, '...*can see without the use of physical eyes. It perceives by intuition. It has the power to communicate with others without the aid of physical means... It receives intelligence and transmits it to people at a distance.*'

In a series of experiments, physicists Harold Puthoff and Russell Targ of California's Stanford Research Institute found that just about everyone they tested had the capacity they termed, 'remote viewing'. Remote viewing is the ability to describe what another person in a different physical location is seeing. Their controversial findings have been successfully replicated by various studies around the world, including an experiment carried out by The Princeton Anomalies Research laboratory. Highly respected physicist Robert Jahn served as the receiver and tried to describe what his colleague in Paris was viewing. Jahn, who had never visited the city, described a bustling street which, let's face it, was hardly surprising. What was strange, however, was that he also described a knight in armour. Meanwhile, his colleague was standing in front of a government building adorned with statues of historical military figures – one of which was a knight in armour.

Hey, look I know what you're thinking – 'That's a bit whacky'. But you must consider that these studies are not coming from crackpot institutions made

> DEFINING IDEA...
> *Intuition comes very close to clairvoyance; it appears to be the extrasensory perception of reality.*
> – DR ALEXIS CARREL, FRENCH SURGEON AND BIOLOGIST

of marshmallow in Somerset, they are originating from some of the world's most prestigious schools. Sceptics would argue there was some trick or false data. Perhaps they are right. However, I myself have witnessed the remarkable abilities of the subconscious mind at work. In fact, various events in my life that make no sense have left me speechless.

I remember staying at a friend's house in Sydney. My friend's boyfriend was becoming increasingly annoyed because he couldn't find the keys for his beloved scooter. I was really tired and quietly getting more and more irritated until finally, I got up out of my beanbag and stormed into another room. There, I went straight to a pair of gloves tucked away on a dresser and shook the gloves – his keys fell out. I remember we all looked at the keys on the floor and no one was more stunned than me. Was it coincidence? Maybe luck? I couldn't have seen him put them there because I'd only just arrived back at the house. In truth, I have no idea how this happened but I'm sure there will come a time when we do understand it.

Collier offers an explanation by saying, 'The subconscious mind supplies the "intuition" that so often carries a woman straight to a point that may require hours of cumbersome reasoning for a man. Even in ordinary, everyday affairs, you often draw upon its wonderful wisdom.' Of course 'intuition' is not sexist – men have it too!

HERE'S AN IDEA FOR YOU...

Investigate the Silva Method. Developed by parapsychologist Jose Silva in the 1940s, the technique claims to increase an individual's IQ and sense of personal well-being by developing their higher brain functions. Silva also believed that practising the method allows you to tap into a higher consciousness, including the ability for remote viewing.

7 COLLECTIVE CONSCIOUSNESS

Collier writes, *'Dr Jung, celebrated Viennese specialist, claims that the subconscious mind contains not only all the knowledge that it has gathered during the life of an individual, but that in addition it contains all the wisdom of past ages.'* Indeed, Swiss psychiatrist Carl Jung's views on collective consciousness are well known.

DEFINING IDEA...
If the brain were so simple we could understand it, we would be so simple we couldn't.
~ LYALL WATSON, ZOOLOGIST AND ANTHROPOLOGIST

What Collier is talking about here is actually now seen as one of the explanations as to why the strange occurrences of the previous chapter are possible. His view was that, 'the subconscious mind is the connecting link between the Creator and us, between Universal Mind and our conscious mind'.

Early in his career Jung became convinced that the dreams, fantasies and hallucinations of his patients contained symbols and insights that could not be explained through their personal history. Instead such symbols more closely resembled the images contained in great mythologies of the world and in effect sprang from the same source – a collective consciousness shared by all people: past, present and future.

The idea of some shared central information source would certainly explain various odd phenomena that have occurred in the natural world. For example, when South African scientist Lyall Watson introduced a new food source – sand-covered sweet potatoes – to a tribe of monkeys on an island near Japan he was surprised to see how fast good news really travelled. Their existing food source didn't require any preparation and so initially the monkeys were reluctant to eat the sandy potatoes. It wasn't long before a female monkey washed the potato; she then taught her mother and playmates to do the same. But then something remarkable happened – all the monkeys in the area started to wash the potatoes. There was no physical way the monkeys could have interacted as they were in different locations on the island and some of them were even on different islands. It is believed that some form of critical mass occurred at an estimated number of 100 monkeys and at that point all the monkeys had access to the knowledge.

Quantum mechanics, however, may offer a simple, though equally whacky explanation. One of the observations of quantum physics is there appeared to be an instantaneous communication between subatomic particles, even if separated by vast distances. It was this aspect of quantum physics that most troubled the great scientist Albert Einstein because it meant the communication was happening faster than the speed of light and his theory of relativity said this was impossible. David Bohm, one of the world's most respected quantum physicists and a protégé of Einstein, suggested a radical explanation, 'Deep down the consciousness of mankind is one.' As such, the particles were not 'communicating' but rather they were connected – that everything is interconnected.

Whatever the solution might be, Collier states, 'That by drawing upon its wisdom and power the individual may possess any good thing of life, from health and happiness to riches and success.'

HERE'S AN IDEA FOR YOU...
If we really are all made of the same stuff vibrating at different frequencies and we are all connected, you may want to think twice about how you treat others because you will experience everything that you dish out.

8 THE AMAZING ABILITIES OF MIND

Collier talks of *'lightning calculators'* – young children who can calculate mathematical problems faster than a calculator or people who listen to a piece of music once and immediately play it perfectly. He refers to their special gifts as part of the subconscious mind. Today, sadly, we would probably label them autistic.

DEFINING IDEA...
The future looks extremely bright indeed, with lots of possibilities ahead – big possibilities. Like the song says, 'We've only just begun…'
~ BRUCE LEE, ACTOR

Temple Grandin is an internationally respected expert in animal behaviour with a doctorate in animal sciences. At the time of writing she is an associate professor at Colorado State University. Grandin has designed cattle handling facilities all over the world. Half the cattle in North America are handled using her designs and she consults to firms such as Burger King and McDonald's. Her unique contribution has made a huge difference to the welfare of cattle, reduced the stress of the animals and led to more humane slaughter. Temple Grandin is also autistic – highly autistic.

Despite a normal birth, by the age of six months Grandin would stiffen at her mother's touch and claw to escape hugs. At three years old, the doctors pronounced she had brain damage and she endured a difficult childhood. By the time she was sixteen, Grandin and her doctors had discovered that she had a photographic memory. She was an autistic savant. She visited her aunt's cattle ranch in Arizona and became fascinated by the cattle crush – a large device with two metal plates that squeezed the animal's sides, relaxing it sufficiently for safe inspection by a veterinary surgeon. Though physical closeness to another person was too overwhelming for her senses, she still craved tactile stimulation and so she decided to build a human crush. The project sparked an interest in mechanical engineering, problem solving and animal behaviour that would change her life. Even better, the device that she built delivered the same calming effect that she had witnessed at the ranch. She gained relief from the machine and was subsequently more empathetic, more in touch with her feelings, even more tolerant of human touch.

Since those early days Grandin has been able to use this and other techniques to rewire her brain and effectively manage her autism, thereby giving inspiration to others.

Extraordinary abilities are frequently accompanied by autism or some other brain disability. One scientist who thinks we all start out as savants, but 'normal' cognitive functioning blocks them is Dr Allan Snyder of the University of Sydney. His theory results from experimentation where he directed a few electromagnetic pulses to the frontal lobe and 40% of his test subjects displayed extraordinary, newfound mental skills. Snyder suggests that such skills as, 'the mental machinery for performing lightning fast integer arithmetic calculations could be within us all.'

Perhaps a tad optimistically, Collier predicts, 'The time will come when, as H. G. Wells envisioned in his *Men Like Gods*, schools and teachers will no longer be necessary except to show us how to get in touch with the infinite knowledge our subconscious minds possess from infancy'.

HERE'S AN IDEA FOR YOU...

Unless you have a transcranial magnetic stimulator handy and someone happy to zap you a few times, you probably won't get the opportunity to be a savant for a day. But the idea that we have latent talents might inspire you to try to find them!

9 YOUR SUBCONSCIOUS NEVER SLEEPS

Collier tells us, *'Your conscious mind may slumber. It may be rendered impotent by anaesthetics or sudden blow. But your subconscious mind works on, keeping your heart and lungs, your arteries and glands ever on the job.'* In other words, the conscious mind sleeps, but the subconscious never does.

DEFINING IDEA...
Whenever a doctor cannot do good, he must be kept from doing harm.
~ HIPPOCRATES

However, the subconscious is not, as Collier suggested, rendered impotent by a sudden blow. For decades, surgeons assumed that unconscious patients were unaware of their surroundings and so they would happily discuss the case in question in the theatre. But studies into this assumption showed not only could the patient recall these discussions, the healing process was influenced by their content. If, for example, a surgeon commented on how bad the particular case was, or when the necessary incisions were made stated aloud that the patient's condition was far worse than expected, then the patient's chance of survival was adversely affected.

Remember when Lipton described the subconscious mind as being a repository for stored information (page 17)? That information spoken by the doctor went straight into the repository and was used to deliver the expected result – even though the patient wasn't conscious of it. The subconscious mind does not decide what is right or wrong, it simply stores information that affects the blueprint of your life.

There are umpteen studies into whether there is a correlation between what is said in the operating theatre and post-operative healing. In one study conducted in New York University Medical Center involving seventy patients undergoing hernia repair, patients who received positive healing suggestions under anaesthetic showed a marked difference from the control group. While there was no difference in post-operative pain, there was a significant reduction in nausea and vomiting as well as other post-operative side effects. However, another study conducted in Swindon of 140 patients undergoing a total hysterectomy showed no difference in pain, post-operative nausea or vomiting between those who received positive suggestions and those who did not.

One theory that may explain the differing results is hinted at by Weinberger, Sternberg and Gold (1984), who reported that adrenaline acted as a switch for turning on memory-formation processes in rats, 'even when they were anesthetized and unconscious'. Therefore, it may be that when someone 'hears' a distressing negative prognosis while unconscious, their subconscious activates the 'Pavlovian' fear or survival response and releases adrenaline, thereby causing the statement to have more impact on the subconscious mind than it otherwise would.

Collier reminds us that, 'Under ordinary conditions [the subconscious mind] attends faithfully to its duties, and leaves your conscious mind to direct the outer life of the body.'

HERE'S AN IDEA FOR YOU...
If you are ever unlucky enough to need surgery that requires you to be unconscious, request that the doctors or surgeons involved stay as silent as possible. Or if they happen to be a believer in positive conditioning, they may even encourage healing by giving you positive affirmations while unconscious.

10 WHAT IS PRAYER?

Collier suggests, *'For mind does its building solely by the power of thought... [which] explains the power of prayer. The results of prayer are not brought about by some special dispensation of Providence. God is not a finite being to be cajoled or flattered into doing as you desire.'*

> DEFINING IDEA...
> *It is vain to expect our prayers to be heard if we do not strive as well as pray.*
> ~ AESOP, GREEK WRITER OF FABLES

I couldn't agree more! In its day, the New Thought movement of which Collier was a part was a type of spirituality or religious belief. Founded by women and based on Unity Church, Religious Science and the Church of Divine Science, many of the initial followers were also women. No surprise then that Collier wrote a great deal about God, especially when you consider that he almost became a priest before heading for West Virginia as a young man to seek his fortune.

Yet he does so in a remarkably refreshing way. If, as is now being proven by various scientists, intention and strongly felt emotional desire somehow impacts on the quantum field to influence the outcome, surely prayer is just another name for that process?

First, the science... physicist William Tiller of Stanford University is a leading figure in the study of intention. In his book, *Conscious Acts of Creation*, he details the rigorous studies that prove our intention and thought influence outcome. He concludes, 'From these studies and more like them, it can be seen that belief fuels expectations and expectations, in turn, marshal intention at both unconscious and conscious levels to fulfil expectations.' Like many great thinkers and scientists before him, Tiller's research has met resistance. He justifies this by saying, 'It's a human characteristic to be comfortable with a certain way of viewing the world. New stuff is uncomfortable; you have to change your way of thinking.'

According to Tiller, 'There is no place in our present paradigm for any form of consciousness, intention, emotion, mind or spirit to enter. And because our work shows that consciousness can have a very robust effect on physical reality and that means that ultimately there must be a paradigm shift.'

Could it be that prayer works not because some omnipotent all-seeing, all-knowing character who resembles Harry Potter's Dumbledore has decided to check in and throw you a bone, but simply because your focused, concentrated thought has made an impression on the subconscious mind and ultimately the pure potentiality of the quantum field? In effect, prayer is nothing more than religious goal setting – a consistent focus on what you desire, using consistent creative visualisation to vividly image the desired outcome.

Collier suggests, 'When you pray earnestly, you form a mental image of the thing that you desire and you hold it strongly in your thought. Then the Universal Intelligence, which is your intelligence – Omnipotent Mind – begins to work with and for you, and this is what brings about the manifestation that you desire.'

HERE'S AN IDEA FOR YOU...
Call it prayer- or goal-setting, the process is the same: decide what you want. Focus on it often and vividly imagine your life having achieved those desires in the present tense. Inject positive energy, excitement and desire into the visualisation.

11 WE CAN DO ONLY WHAT WE THINK WE CAN DO

Collier states, '... *life is the result of our mental attitude. We can do only what we think we can do. We can be only what we think we can be. We can have only what we think we can have. [It] all depends upon what we think.*'

What Collier may not have appreciated then is the powerful role that other people's attitudes have on your results.

DEFINING IDEA...

Drugs are not always necessary, but belief in recovery always is.
– NORMAN COUSINS, WRITER AND ADVOCATE OF HOLISTIC HEALING

When Dr Albert Mason was asked to treat a fifteen-year-old boy who had a bad case of warts using hypnosis in 1952, he jumped at the chance. As a skilled hypnotist, he'd had many successes with similar cases. Apart from his chest, the boy's entire body was affected and his skin was thick and leathery as a result. While in hypnotic trance, Mason told the boy that his skin would heal and turn healthy and pink like his chest. The treatment worked, with most of the boy's skin returning to normal. Mason then took the boy to the referring surgeon, who was wide-eyed in astonishment.

However, Mason had been misinformed for the boy was, in fact, suffering from a lethal genetic disease – congenital ichthyosis. His hypnosis had achieved the impossible and the achievement created a sensation and made him a magnet for rare and supposedly untreatable diseases, yet he was unable to replicate the same healing. Mason himself attributed his failure to his own belief about the treatment. He had thought the boy had warts and so he was super-confident that he could treat the condition, thereby healing him. Once he knew that the boy had an incurable genetic condition, his belief dissolved and therefore his attitude changed, making it impossible to achieve the results.

And what of Sam Londe, who was diagnosed with cancer of the oesophagus in 1974, at a time when the condition was considered 100% fatal? Unsurprisingly to those involved in the case, Sam died a few weeks after diagnosis. What was more surprising, though, was that the autopsy found very little cancer in his body – certainly not enough to kill him. His physician Clifton Meador commented, 'He died with cancer, but not from cancer.' More than thirty years on, the case still haunts Meador, 'I thought he had cancer. He thought he had cancer. Everyone around him thought he had cancer... Did I remove hope in some way?' As Bruce Lipman states in his book, *The Biology of Belief*, 'Nocebo cases suggest that physicians, parents and teachers can remove hope by programming you to believe you are powerless.'

Collier adds, 'William James, the famous psychologist, said that the greatest discovery in a hundred years was the discovery of the subconscious mind... It is the discovery that man has within himself the power to control his surroundings.' True, but how do you control other's thoughts and stop them influencing you? You must protect yourself from the negative attitudes and expectations of others – even though it's not that easy sometimes!

HERE'S AN IDEA FOR YOU...

If you have a pessimistic doctor – find a different one! No one knows the future and life expectancy predictions are merely opinion that is all too often taken as fact and turned into a personal death sentence. Don't ever let that happen to you or someone you love.

12 A LITTLE BIT OF PHYSICS

According to Collier, an article in the *New York Tribune* on 11 March 1926 stated, *'We used to believe that the universe was composed of an unknown number of different kinds of matter, one for each element.'* But, says Collier, *'that romantic prospect no longer exists.'*

DEFINING IDEA...
Those who are not shocked when they first come across quantum theory cannot possibly have understood it.
~ NIELS BOHR, NOBEL PRIZE-WINNING QUANTUM PHYSICIST

Instead there were only two – a negative electron and a positive proton: 'From these protons and electrons all the chemical elements are built up. Iron and lead and oxygen and gold and all the others differ from one another merely in the nature and arrangement of the electrons and protons, which they contain. This is the modern idea of the nature of matter. Matter is really nothing but electricity.'

Believe it or not, this view still largely holds true. As science has been able to explore the minutiae of the universe and go inside the atom and down to the subatomic level, less and less has been found. Philosopher and theologian Dr Miceal Ledwith proposes that the modern scientific views which attempt to uncover these mysteries indicate, 'reality is not solid, it's mostly empty space and whatever solidity it has seems more to resemble a hologram picture rather than solid harsh reality. It's a shimmering reality that seems to be very susceptible to the power of thought.'

Much of this new research comes from the mind-boggling world of quantum physics. Richard Feynman, 1965 Nobel Prize winner for the development of quantum electrodynamics, said, 'I think I can safely say that nobody understands quantum mechanics.' I for one certainly don't! But the crux of it is the smaller we go, the more empty space there is. Populating that space are particles – and they aren't solid either. The same particle can be in numerous different places at once and they move instantaneously, implying an even deeper connection we are not yet aware of. In addition, these particles alter their behaviour from particle to wave depending on what the scientist expects. This fluidity of characteristics makes them impossible to predict and the very act of observation alters them so we don't really know what the universe is doing when our back is turned! Some have suggested that when it's unwatched or unmeasured, the world is simply a fuzzy 'probability field' which 'collapses' into solid reality only when observed.

So, what does it mean? To put it simply, your thoughts and emotions impress themselves on the quantum probability field to create what you experience as reality. Or, as William Tiller puts it, 'We are running the Holodeck. It has such flexibility that anything you can imagine it will create for you. Your intention causes this thing to materialise once you're conscious enough, and you learn how to use your intentionality.'

If you don't like this idea, you might want to consider changing your thoughts and emotions.

HERE'S AN IDEA FOR YOU...

If you are interested in knowing more about quantum physics but don't know where to start, watch the documentary, What the Bleep Do We Know!? *Part story, part science lesson, the DVD takes you on a layman's journey of physics, spirituality, neurology and evolutionary thought.*

13 DON'T THINK OF ABRACADABRA

Collier tells the tale of a *'shrewd necromancer'*, who told the King that he had discovered a way to make gold out of sand. The King offered a great reward for the knowledge – all the King had to do during the simple process was *not* to think of the word, 'Abracadabra'.

Although this little story may sound slightly random, it is perhaps one of the most important points in the entire book. Although unaware of it, most people already put the awesome manifesting power of their mind to work – it's just that they are creating what they don't want!

Writer Fyodor Dostoevsky illuminated this idea when he wrote in *Winter Notes on Summer Impressions*, 'Try to pose for yourself this task: not to think of a polar bear and you will see that the cursed thing will come to mind every minute.'

DEFINING IDEA...
To a great extent, we find what we look for.
~ ROBERT COLLIER

So, what's your 'polar bear'? If intense, emotional thought impresses the quantum probability field to manifest your reality, what intense, emotional thoughts are you harbouring on a regular basis? Are you focused on all the great things you want to achieve in your life, or are your thoughts churning because your teenage daughter has discovered boys and wants to grow up a little too quickly? Maybe you're excited about the future or worried about your job, the economy, your bills, your business and the chances of survival?

The sad fact of everyday life is that most of us spend much of our thinking time and energy worrying about what we don't want to happen! That quantum probability field doesn't care what it manifests. If your thoughts and actions are focused on your worries and all the stuff you don't want, then unless you have some powerful contradictory beliefs already programmed into your subconscious (unlikely), you will actively bring about the very situations that you fear.

Psychologists at the University of Western Australia proved that it is futile to tell someone not to think of something. In their first study they asked students to watch videos of Australian Rules football. Students asked not to pay attention to the umpire actually increased their awareness of him. In the second study, however, half the students were given a cue word to refocus their thinking away from the umpire, when needed. Even under highly distractive conditions, the students performed better at the task when they used a word to refocus, thereby proving that we need to start to refocus our thoughts on the positive and break the pattern of negative thinking.

As Collier reminds us, 'To be ambitious for wealth and yet always expecting to be poor; to be always doubting your ability to get what you long for is like trying to reach east by travelling west. There is no philosophy which will help a man to succeed when he always doubts his ability to do so.'

HERE'S AN IDEA FOR YOU...

Create some fun cue words that you can yell out when you find yourself worrying about things you don't want to happen. You may not be able to yell them out all the time, but if you choose a stupid word such as 'collywobbles', hopefully this will also make you laugh out loud and that too can break your negative thinking.

14 GARBAGE IN, GARBAGE OUT

Collier says, *'Thought externalizes itself. What we are depends entirely upon the images we hold before our mind's eye. Every time we think, we start a chain of causes, which will create conditions similar to the thoughts, which originated it.'* If that doesn't scare you, perhaps it should!

> DEFINING IDEA...
> *Laughter and tears are both responses to frustration and exhaustion... I myself prefer to laugh, since there is less cleaning up to do afterwards.*
> – KURT VONNEGUT, NOVELIST

Back in the 1920s, when Collier wrote *The Secret of the Ages*, there was no TV, let alone 24-hour TV. The newspapers reported news instead of opinion and sensationalism. Collier encouraged his readers to put good stuff into their minds, surround themselves with positive people and make plans to pursue their dreams with a singleness of purpose. After all, what else could you do at night?

Today is a very different world, in which billions start their day with an avalanche of bad news delivered by a warped media bulging with vested interests and political agenda. Terrorism or usually, alleged terrorism, another senseless murder, knife crime and gang violence, rising unemployment, continued recession, escalating casualties in Afghanistan, while fat-cat bankers purr as they inflict record profit margins on struggling borrowers despite being largely to blame for bringing the global financial sector to its knees, politicians' expense scandals and swine flu.

How do you feel about the injustice, violence, greed and hypocrisy? Is it likely to set up thinking that will start a good or bad chain of causes? Will that negativity be likely to affect your day and influence the effects it creates? Of course it will! Then, after work you come home to relax. You watch 'Mope' operas where everyone is miserable, lurching from one unrealistic disaster to the next or s**tcoms. Or perhaps you watch a film or play a computer game – only they are full of violence too. Recently, I was bamboozled while watching a TV programme highlighting just how many young people get their sex education from pornography, in which boys were deciding if their tackle was 'normal' based on that benchmark!

This is scary, not because of some moral judgement but because all this stuff seeps into the subconscious mind. Collier says, 'When you can direct your thought processes you can consciously apply them to any condition, for all that comes to us from the world without is what we've already imagined in the world within.'

So what are people imagining as a result of the new technology? In computer games or Internet environments such as Second Life, users can make their Avatar do anything, from getting married to rape and child abuse! To think that these things do not negatively affect the development process, influence thinking, imagination and ultimately action in the real world, is wildly naive. However, Collier gives us hope when he states, 'All power is from within and is therefore under our own control'. Maybe it's time we started using it!

HERE'S AN IDEA FOR YOU...
Don't read newspapers and don't watch the news – certainly not in the morning. If you must, get the headlines and then turn the TV off. If you do watch television, choose something uplifting, interesting or educational.

15 UNUSED TALENT DECAYS

Collier suggests that if you are beginning to appreciate the power within you then you must, *'begin at once, today, to use what you have learned. All growth comes from a particle. All the forces of life are active – peace – joy – power; the unused talent decays.'* In other words, use it or lose it!

DEFINING IDEA...
Iron rusts from disuse, stagnant water loses its purity and in cold weather becomes frozen; even so does inaction sap the vigors of the mind.
~ LEONARDO DA VINCI, ARTIST AND INVENTOR

The brain is made up of two types of cells, neurons and glia, and it's pretty much complete at the eighth month of pregnancy, with twice as many neurons as the adult version. As we age neurons that aren't used, don't fit the required job or are simply too weak will be pruned away in a process known as 'Neural Darwinism'. Therefore, the assumption is that as we age, our capacity to learn and retain information diminishes, but it's not true. If you don't use your brain, then of course you will lose it but that has nothing to do with age!

In truth, the brain is much more pliable than we first thought. It is able to change as our environment and experiences change; we can learn and more importantly, unlearn! Whenever you carry out certain behaviour or think a thought a neural pathway is created. If that behaviour or thought is repeated often enough the pathway becomes more fixed and turns into a neural superhighway. When those superhighways are positive, it's great! If not, they can be very destructive but they can be dismantled.

Your brain has amazing plasticity. Did you know, for example that the brain can retrain idle networks to carry out new tasks? People who have suffered brain damage have been able to retrain other parts of their brain to do what the damaged part used to do and this basic plasticity remains, regardless of age. Your brain can renew itself, learn and rewire and you don't need to sit in a classroom to do so – it is possible through new thought, new actions and new emotions.

Researchers divided a test group into four. The first group were asked to physically practise a one-handed five-finger exercise on the piano. Group two were to play the piano randomly and group three were asked to watch group one, memorise the exercise and mentally rehearse it only while group four did nothing. Each group was to do their thing for two hours a day, for five days. Two things were fascinating about this study: first, the speed at which the brain altered – new pathways were created after just ten hours of practise over five days. Perhaps what is even more amazing is that group three, who did not actually play the piano, but pretended to do so in their minds had almost as much brain activity in the exact same area of the brain as group one!

Collier reminds us, 'You share in that all-power, all-wisdom of Mind… But you've got to take it. The power is there – but you must use it.'

HERE'S AN IDEA FOR YOU...
Make a pact with yourself that you will try something new every week. If you have children, make this a family mission and ensure that your family is exposed to as many different experiences and viewpoints as possible.

16 A FAIRY-WISHING RING

Collier asks, *'If you had a fairy-wishing ring, what one thing would you wish for? Wealth? Honor? Fame? Love? What one thing do you desire above everything else in life... Whatever you desire wholeheartedly, with singleness of purpose – you can have'.* Only it sounds much easier than it really is.

The problem is that most of us don't have a clue what we'd do with a fairy-wishing ring, especially one that required a single wish!

DEFINING IDEA...

Men try to run life according to their wishes; life runs itself according to necessity.
– JEAN TOOMER, US POET

Most probably, the uninspired would choose 'to be wealthy', but money is not the source of happiness – just ask some of the miserable lottery jackpot winners! It's true that too little cash can cause unhappiness, but having enough works just as well as obscene wealth. Besides, according to Adam Smith in his book, *The Theory of Moral Sentiments*, the insatiable desire to make lots of money is a mental disease. Wealthy industrialist Andrew Carnegie agreed, saying, 'Man must have an idol and the amassing of wealth is one of the worst species of idolatry! No idol is more debasing than the worship of money!'

So, let's forget money. What would you ask your fairy-wishing ring for now? Stumped? It's tricky, isn't it? How do you work out what that singleness of purpose is? And how can we help our children to work out what they are particularly good at and find ways to appreciate the wide spectrum of talents that exist outside the usual academic confinement?

There is more to knowledge than the National Curriculum. In fact, it's often confused me that the really important stuff, such as money management, communication skills and relationships, are not taught in school, unlike trigonometry! Fact is, there are a myriad of talents outside the accepted definition of intelligence. One man of the view that compulsory schooling does more to hinder and obscure those talents than nurture them is John Taylor Gatto. His brilliant work is made all the more insightful and distressing when you consider that he was a schoolteacher for over 30 years. In his 2009 book, *Weapons of Mass Instruction*, he reminds us that the founding fathers of education, 'didn't want brains or talent, just obedience'.

School doesn't encourage you to find your difference and exploit your unique abilities, it urges you to conform to similarity and obscure them. That's why most adults haven't got a clue what they want to do. And yet without an appreciation of your innate gifts, it's very difficult to find a single purpose and without that, you'll have wishy-washy dreams with wishy-washy results.

Collier reminds us, 'Most men jog along in a rut, going through the same old routine day after day, eking out a bare livelihood with no definite desire other than a vague hope that fortune will some day drop in their lap. Fortune doesn't often play such pranks. And a rut, you know, differs from a grave only in depth'.

HERE'S AN IDEA FOR YOU...

Ask your parents or childhood friends what you wanted to be when you grew up. What you initially wanted to do often illustrates an innate desire or interest that you may have since forgotten about. Ask your parents for any memories that may act as a starting point for investigation.

17 MENTAL BROWNIES

According to Collier, *'To use your mind to the best advantage doesn't mean to toil along with the mere conscious part of it. It means hitching up your conscious mind with the Man Inside You, with the little "mental brownies" as Robert Louis Stevenson called them.'*

Apparently Stevenson was very fond of his 'mental brownies', adding, 'My Brownies! God bless them! [They] do one-half of my work for me when I am fast asleep and in all human likelihood do the rest for me as well when I am wide awake and foolishly suppose that I do it myself.'

> DEFINING IDEA...
> *All the resources we need are in the mind.*
> – THEODORE ROOSEVELT, 26TH US PRESIDENT

Rather disturbingly perhaps, I know exactly what he's talking about. When I'm ghostwriting a book, for example, I am often given the author's prior attempts at the manuscript and usually this is not much more than a brain dump. I don't know how it happens, but I start rearranging the material into sections, cutting and pasting madly. Often, I'm not even really that aware of where things are going and yet as I go back to review it, the material is presented in an ideal sequence. Perhaps that's what Stevenson is talking about – it's a state of flow, where I get out of the way and something else takes over; I am a bystander to a different process that I don't consciously control. Perhaps this is similar to 'the Zone' that athletes talk about, when everything comes together for optimal performance.

Collier tells how, 'every man who has a problem to solve has had like experiences. You know how, after you have studied a problem from all angles,

MENTAL BROWNIES

it somehow seems worse jumbled than when you started on it. Leave it for a while – forget it – and when you go back to it, you find your thoughts clarified.'

Writing this book, I had this exact same experience. As I read *The Secret of the Ages* for the first time, I made post-it notes at all the bits I found particularly interesting. Stevenson's 'mental brownies' made me laugh and I also wrote, 'cartoon with little people in head' on my post-it. But try as I might, I just couldn't remember their name. All I could remember was this was a cartoon that I watched as a child, so I forgot about it and as I sat down to write this chapter, the 'brownies' came through in style: 'The Numbskulls'! It was a comic strip that first appeared in *The Beano* about the adventures of six 'Numbskulls' – Alf, Fred, Luggy, Cruncher, Snitch and Brainy, who lived inside a man's head and controlled his actions!

So, whenever you are stressed or confused about anything, consider handing over the task to your mental brownies or Numbskulls, if you prefer, for 'they are willing to assist us in our mental work, if we will but have confidence and trust in them'.

HERE'S AN IDEA FOR YOU...

If you can't remember something, make a note of it on a post-it by your bed. Ask the question before you go to sleep and then forget it. Have a pen and paper at the ready as you may get a flash of inspiration in the middle of the night or as you wake up.

18 THE LAW OF VISUALISATION

Collier suggests, *'There is a very real law of cause and effect, which makes the dream of the dreamer come true. It is the law of visualisation – the law that calls into being in this outer material world everything that is real in the inner world...'*

You may have heard of visualisation or mental rehearsal before. Although it is talked about extensively in ancient spiritual texts, visualisation is in fact best known as a tool to improve sporting performance.

> DEFINING IDEA...
> *To accomplish great things we must first dream, then visualize, then plan... believe... act!*
> ~ ALFRED A. MONTAPERT, AUTHOR

It was the Soviets who did the initial groundwork in the subject and their interest in the possibility of visualisation came from an unlikely source – the Soviet Space programme. Doctor and researcher Alexander Romen's area of speciality was the influence of self-suggestion on the human body and in the 1950s he searched for ways to allow cosmonauts to handle emotionally challenging situations in space. His method involved active self-suggestion and was drawn from elements of Zen, Yoga, Chinese medicine, autogenic training and progressive relaxation.

In his book, *Peak Performance*, former NASA researcher and US authority on high achievement Charles Garfield wrote of meeting Soviet sports psychologists in Milan three years after the Montreal Olympic Games, where they topped the medal table with 125 medals, including 49 gold.

The sports psychologists told Garfield about sophisticated mental training techniques that run parallel to rigorous physical training. In one study, four groups of world-class athletes of matched ability were put through their paces for many hours each week. The training programme was slightly different for each group:

- Group I – 100% physical training
- Group II – 75% physical training and 25% mental training
- Group III – 50% physical training and 50% mental training
- Group IV – 25% physical training and 75% mental training

When the four groups were assessed prior to their departure for the 1980 Winter Olympics in Lake Placid, Group IV showed the greatest improvement, followed (in order) by Group III, Group II and finally, Group I.

In their enthusiasm to share their findings the Soviet psychologists put Garfield himself through their visualisation process and he bench-pressed 165.5 kg (365 lb) – way above the 127 kg (280 lb) most recently managed by him. Garfield said, 'The imagery now imprinted in my mind began to guide my physical movements. Slowly and patiently, their voices sure yet gentle, the Soviets led me through the lift. I became convinced I could do it. The world around me seemed to fade, giving way to self-confidence, belief in myself, and then to deliberate action. I lifted the weight! I was absolutely astounded.'

Collier reminds us to, 'Make your mental image clear enough, picture it vividly in every detail, and the genie-of-your-mind will speedily bring it into being as an everyday reality.' I'm not totally convinced of the speedy part, but visualisation is certainly a powerful tool in harnessing the power of your subconscious to realise your desires.

HERE'S AN IDEA FOR YOU...
Cut out images of the things you want and create a goal-board with them. Place this in your bedroom so that you see it last thing at night and first thing in the morning. Now take a moment to imagine having achieved all those things.

19 IT'S THE LITTLE THINGS THAT COUNT

Collier refers to the idea that lots of little things eventually turn into big things – *'A skyscraper is built from individual bricks.'* He quotes Professor James (presumably William James) as saying: *'We become permanent drunkards by so many separate drinks.'* Although not a particularly positive example, it's an accurate one.

DEFINING IDEA...
Success in life is founded upon attention to the small things rather than to the large things; to the everyday things nearest to us rather than to the things that are remote and uncommon.
~ BOOKER T. WASHINGTON, EDUCATOR, AUTHOR AND ORATOR

In *The Tipping Point*, Malcolm Gladwell tells the story of Brownsville, a New York City neighbourhood that was suddenly and miraculously transformed by little things. Come dusk, Brownsville was a ghost town and synonymous with the drug trade and gang warfare. In 1992, there were 2,154 murders in New York and 626,182 serious crimes and Brownsville featured heavily in those statistics. Then something happened… Crime rates reversed and within five years, murders dropped by 64.3% and total crime figures had almost halved.

The police said this was due to improved policing strategies, while criminologists pointed to the decline in crack cocaine and an ageing population. Economists put it down to more people being employed, but none of those theories explains the dramatic reduction. Gladwell says, 'Crime didn't taper off. It didn't decelerate. It hit a certain point and jammed on the brakes.'

Why did this happen? One explanation is the 'broken window' theory. Brainchild of the criminologists James Wilson and George Kelling, the broken window theory argues crime is the inevitable result of disorder. If a little thing like a window is broken and left that way, it is assumed that no one cares and no one's in charge. Soon, more windows become broken and that sends out a strong message that anything goes. Wilson and Kelling propose relatively minor things, such as graffiti, public disorder and aggressive begging, are equivalent to broken window and act as an invitation to more serious crime. In the mid-1980s, Kelling was hired as a consultant by the New York Transit Authority and urged them to put the broken window theory into practice, and so they did. Graffiti was persistently removed from subway cars and there was a crackdown on fare beating. It is thought that this attention to the little things snowballed, resulting in the sudden decline in crime.

Of the other theories that persist the most interesting comes from the book *Freakonomics*. Authors Steven D. Levitt and Stephen J. Dubner propose the real reason crime dropped so dramatically was because some 20 years earlier abortion became legal in the US. Until 22 January 1973 women were forced to endure the horror of illegal abortion or have children that they didn't want and couldn't care for either. Decades of studies showed that a child born under those circumstances was far more likely than any other to turn to crime. So the crime rate dropped dramatically because those who would have been committing the offences were no longer being born!

While the truth is most probably a combination of many factors, there can be little doubt as to the power of little things.

HERE'S AN IDEA FOR YOU...
Whether you are running a business or running a home, take care of the little things. Don't let the little things slide or they will turn into big issues.

20 THE DANGER OF 'TRUTH'

Collier states, *'In our great-grandfather's day, when witches flew around by night and cast their spell upon all unlucky enough to cross them, men thought that the power of sickness or health, of good fortune or ill, resided outside himself or herself.'*

In days past, when we did not understand the laws of nature, we believed in witches and curses. There are still parts of the world where people continue to do so and sometimes 'truth' can be dangerous.

> DEFINING IDEA...
> *The truth is often a terrible weapon of aggression. It is possible to lie, and even to murder for the truth.*
> – ALFRED ALDER, PSYCHOLOGIST

When the lifelong brain disorder Autism was first diagnosed, it was blamed on unemotional parents, especially mothers! Not only were the family beside themselves because their beloved child was somehow different, but they were blamed for it too! Thankfully that particular 'truth' has been rectified, but some are harder to kill. At times, science is as keen to dismiss exceptions as religion and both to the detriment of society as a whole.

Take 'germ theory', which is attributed – some say unfairly – to the French chemist and biologist Louis Pasteur. Germ theory states bacteria and viruses are the cause of disease. One of germ theory's most passionate critics was the French physiologist Claude Bernard (1813–78). So convinced was he that it was wrong that he said, 'The terrain is everything; the germ is nothing,' and then promptly drank a glass of water laced with the cholera! To everyone's astonishment, he remained completely unaffected despite this being a virulent pathogen. Describing this incident, a *Science* article published in 2000 states, 'For unexplained reasons he remained symptom-free, but nevertheless incorrect.'

If Bernard didn't become sick then germ theory must be incorrect – or at least incomplete. Yet this idea is still very much alive and kicking today.

Another great white hope that is turning into a white elephant is genetics. Here, we are mapped and tagged to within an inch of our lives, but what does it actually tell us? Not that much!

The new science of Epigenics (meaning 'control above the genes') shows that our genetic make-up is not set in stone to deliver foregone conclusion after biological foregone conclusion. Environmental signals select, modify and regulate gene activity, which means that genes are constantly remodelled in response to life experiences.

There are now cases of young healthy women having their breasts removed because they have a genetic disposition to breast cancer. Yet science proves that your genes are not your destiny. Sadly the media love a good story and they don't get much juicier than sensational links between genes and disease. The press went wild, for example, over the discovery of the BRCA1 and the BRCA2 breast cancer genes, but failed to emphasise that 95% of breast cancers are not due to inherited genes.

Collier says, 'We image thoughts upon our subconscious minds and the genie-of-our-mind finds a way of bringing them into effect. The mental image is what counts. Be it good or ill.'

HERE'S AN IDEA FOR YOU...
For every theory there is an alternate and opposite theory – truth is therefore largely subjective. Before you accept anything as fact, you must decide if that belief helps or hinders you.

21 IT'S WRITTEN ALL OVER YOUR FACE

Collier says, 'A man with an ugly disposition (which is a mental state) will have harsh, unlovely features. One with a gentle disposition will have a smiling and serene countenance... Fear, irritability and hate distort the features.' In other words, your thoughts and feelings are written all over your face.

DEFINING IDEA...

A man finds room in the few square inches of his face for the traits of all his ancestors; for the expression of all his history, and his wants.
~ RALPH WALDO EMERSON,
US PHILOSPHER AND POET

I must admit that there isn't much TV that I enjoy, but *Lie to Me* is an exception. The series is centred on the exploits of deception specialist Dr Cal Lightman, played brilliantly by Tim Roth. What makes the show especially enjoyable is that it is based on the real-world science of clinical psychologist, and human lie detector Dr Paul Ekman, who is the scientific advisor on the show.

Ekman's research indicates that our facial expressions are innate, universal and almost impossible to conceal. Regardless of nationality, language or culture, emotion is expressed in the same way. You might think that you are hiding how you truly feel, but a person who is skilled like Ekman in the detection and interpretation of 'micro expressions' can see the truth written all over your face.

Micro expressions are an instinctive reflex of truth that are a fifteenth to a twenty-fifth of a second long and are involuntarily made before you can cover your emotional tracks. But Ekman's work is not just entertaining: the science of reading facial expressions is a very useful skill, especially for those seeking to find liars. As such, Ekman has advised law enforcement agencies, such as the US Secret Service and the Department of Defense.

What we think and how we feel have a profound effect on the body. Mind and body is a two-way system communicated 24/7 through thought and emotion. Those conversations are written all over your face, resulting in an ugly or gentle disposition.

Collier says, 'Mortals are healthy or unhealthy, happy or unhappy, strong or weak, alive or dead, in the proportions that they think thoughts of health or illness, strength or weakness.' His comments remind me of an exercise that I once did in a workshop. Try it for yourself: ask your partner or kids to help you with the experiment. One of you is A, the other B. Person A holds their arm straight out at the side while person B attempts to push the arm down by applying pressure to their wrist. This establishes 'base-line strength'.

After a moment's rest, repeat the process – only this time person A must quickly repeat out loud, 'I am weak' twenty times – and then person B should attempt to push down the arm again.

Repeat again after a moment's rest only this time person A should repeat out loud, 'I am strong' twenty times before person B tests for strength. The results for many are remarkably different and act as a simple demonstration of the impact thoughts and feelings have on the body. As sixteenth US president Abraham Lincoln once rightly pointed out, 'Every man over forty is responsible for his face.'

HERE'S AN IDEA FOR YOU...
Our emotions have a physical effect on our internal and external landscape and thus form the cartography of our appearance. Eventually, you will look as you think, so think happy thoughts!

22 TAKE THE PEBBLE OUT OF YOUR BOOT

Collier says, *'If a pebble in our boot torments us, we expel it. We take off the boot and shake it out. And once the matter is fairly understood, it is just as easy to expel an intruding and obnoxious thought from the mind.'* Indeed, learning how to stop worrying is a skill worth mastering.

There are two reasons why learning to remove the mental irritants from your life is so important. First, worrying isn't that much fun and it doesn't make for a happy and fulfilled life, unless you are one of those people who are only truly happy when they are complaining.

DEFINING IDEA...
When one devotes oneself to meditation, mental burdens, unnecessary worries, and wandering thoughts drop off one by one; life seems to run smoothly and pleasantly.
~ NYOGEN SENZAKILL RANZAI, ZEN MONK

The second point is that science and spirituality has established that thought has a direct and very tangible effect on outcome, especially when that thought is turbo-charged with emotion. Sadly, most of the emotional, passionate and vivid thinking we do is worrying. Worrying about the kids, the bills, your job, the recession, the weather, your parents, the economy, the business, whatever… Worry tends to be packed with juicy emotion. And it is that which impacts the quantum field and affects what we experience in life.

One way to gaining more control over your mind is through meditation. I have always loved the idea of meditation, but never managed to practise regularly. Part of the problem was that I used to equate meditation with some serious, esoteric discipline that required me to sit cross-legged, chanting mantras for hours on end! Seriously, who has the time for that? It was Dan Millman in his book, *Everyday Enlightenment*, who clarified the subject for me and offered a different perspective, 'Sitting meditation is no more and no less inherently spiritual than paying attention to how you walk, eat, breathe, exercise, make love or tie your shoes. In fact, the essence of meditation, of enlightenment, is paying attention.' That's why meditation seems so foreign when we first practise it – rarely do we pay attention to just one thing for any length of time.

You'll never achieve complete silence, that's not the aim. Meditation just gives you greater control over your thoughts so that when they inevitably bubble up from your subconscious, you can seize on them for contemplation if you want to or simply allow them to pass on by. Insomnia is not the inability to sleep – it's the inability to stop thinking. The person struggling to get to sleep is caught in an endless loop of thought that gathers momentum; they can't 'turn off'.

Collier reminds us, 'It should be as easy to expel an obnoxious thought from the mind as to shake a stone out of your shoe; and until a man can do that, it is just nonsense to talk about his ascendancy over nature, and all the rest of it. He is a mere slave, and a prey to the bat-winged phantoms that flit through the corridors of his mind.'

HERE'S AN IDEA FOR YOU...
If you find the sitting meditation difficult, start with walking meditation: just walk, empty your mind and when thoughts arrive, allow them to pass through your mind. Pull your attention back to your breathing, if thoughts interrupt you.

23 THINKING VS ASSOCIATION

Collier encourages us to, *'...think constructively. Don't say you are thinking when all you are doing is exercising your faculty of memory.'* With thinking, the additional challenge is that often we think we are thinking when we are simply activating a conditioned response or long-forgotten, knee-jerk reaction.

When you buy a new computer, the software is pre-loaded with default settings, so in a word processing package sold in the UK, the default language will be English, the margins, tabs etc. will also be defined. Unless you know these can be changed, you will simply assume that's the way it is and accept it.

DEFINING IDEA...
Many a man fails as an original thinker simply because his memory is too good.
~ FRIEDRICH NIETZSCHE, GERMAN PHILOSOPHER

Your brain is the same. By the time you reach adulthood, you have hundreds of thousands of default settings designed to keep you safe and speed up learning. As we grow up, we learn to make sense of the world by a process of association. Everything is logged in detail so that we can use it in future to make 'decisions'. Some highly emotional (good or bad) experiences cause instant learning, such as burning your hand on a naked flame. Other learning develops through repetition in a process called Hebbian learning, after neuropsychologist Donald Hebb who presented the theory in 1949. Clusters of neurons that are repeatedly stimulated grow stronger and into those neural superhighways we mentioned in Chapter 15 (page 38). In essence, nerve cells that fire together, wire together. You create neural habits or default setting.

So, imagine you are an adult and your friend asks if you want to go to Wales for a weekend's camping. Immediately you say no. Later in the week, you get to thinking about it and wonder why you said no – you don't have anything else on that weekend and it would probably be fun. The reason you said no, however, is that you were not thinking when you answered. An old association of Wales and/or camping was triggered and your default setting responded, not your conscious mind.

This associative learning process is great because it allows us to use what we 'know' to learn something new and to keep it safe, but it's also blunt and often inaccurate. Just because you had a bad experience camping as a child or you happened to be chased by a dog when you last visited Wales doesn't mean that the new experience will be bad. What we think is thinking is not actually thinking at all, but the activation of an unconscious habitual response.

Collier quotes from Dumont (probably William Walker Atkinson, who wrote under the pseudonym Theron Q Demont) when we says that most people, 'are simply allowing the stream of memory to flow through their field of consciousness, while the ego stands on the banks and idly watches the passing waters of memory flow by. They call this "thinking", while in reality there is no process of thought under way.'

HERE'S AN IDEA FOR YOU...
Next time you rush for a solution or jump to a conclusion, ask yourself whether you have got all the facts. Is it possible that you are not deciding at all, but simply reacting in the way that you have always reacted to similar situations?

24 SEEK GROWTH – BUT AVOID THE GOLDEN HANDCUFFS

Collier states, *'Don't be satisfied merely because your salary is being boosted occasionally. Learn something every day. When you reach the point in your work that you are no longer adding to your store of knowledge or abilities, you are going backward, and it is time for you to move.'*

What excellent advice! Yet few people have the luxury of viewing their job in this light and the reason for this is the advent and subsequent addiction to credit.

When Collier published his book in 1926, people had to earn *before* they spent and they would save up to make purchases. Today saving is virtually non-existent and we habitually spend way beyond our means.

DEFINING IDEA...

The purpose of learning is growth, and our minds, unlike our bodies, can continue growing as we continue to live.

– MORTIMER J. ADLER, US PHILOSOPHER

According to Credit Action, the total credit card debt in June 2009 was £54.5 billion. The UK collective credit card limit is a whopping £158 billion! It would seem we are very accustomed to spending more than we make. During June 2009, Britain's personal debt increased by £1 million every 108 minutes. And if you think that's staggering, in January 2008 (before the sh*t really hit the global financial fan) Britain's personal debt increased by £1 million every 5.3 minutes!

Sadly, this overspending means the primary purpose of our job is to remain financially afloat. Fulfilment, enjoyment and growth simply don't enter the equation. And then there is the golden handcuffs.

Golden handcuffs replace the gold watch that you would have once received after twenty-five years of service. Instead, as you progress up the corporate ladder you become bound to the job, not through loyalty or passion but the need to service your rising debt.

The scenario goes something like this: you get a promotion, you feel you deserve a treat and so you indulge in some 'retail therapy' – you need to look the part, after all. Now you are moving up in the organisation, you must trade in your old car and get a shiny new one – just to make sure that everyone else knows you are doing well. Over the years, as the promotions come and go, you trade up to a bigger house, faster car, better holidays and designer labels. Only your salary isn't that good! Now you are shackled to a job you hate, but you can't leave because you need the salary just to meet your debts. You have no net worth. This state is aptly called, 'looking good – going nowhere!' What's the point of it? As your income has grown, so too has your expenses and you are no better off than you were when you left school or graduated from university.

Collier reminds us that, 'the biggest salary won't do you much good for long unless you've got the knowledge inside you to back it up'. And it's worth noting that it won't be much good if you are up to your eyes in debt either!

HERE'S AN IDEA FOR YOU...

Collier suggests that every position of employment should yield you three things: reasonable pay for the present, knowledge, training or experience that will be worth money to you in the future and prestige or acquaintances that will be of assistance to you in attaining your goals.

25 ON MARRIAGE

Apparently when a girl is *'picking a husband'* she should go for brains, not money! If she chooses money, *'she'll have a high time for a little while, ending in divorce'*. If brains, *'the start will be hard, but she is likely to end up with a happy home she helped to build…'*

DEFINING IDEA…
Before marriage, a man will go home and lie awake all night thinking about something you said; after marriage, he'll go to sleep before you finished saying it.
~ HELEN ROWLAND, US JOURNALIST AND HUMOURIST

Indeed, Collier adds that, 'money ought to be a consideration in marriage – but never the consideration'. Sadly that's about the extent of his hot tips when it comes to choosing a partner in life. One can only assume that 'beauty' is interchangeable with 'money' when a man is picking a wife! 'When it's a choice of money or brains – take the brains every time. Possessions are of slight importance compared to mind.'

So, what makes a happy marriage? Surely it's not down to such simple choices as money, brains or beauty? John Gottman, who is known for his work on marital stability and relationships, has put forward an interesting theory on compatibility and likelihood of survival. Since the 1980s, he has interviewed more than 3,000 couples in a small room he calls the 'love lab', near the University of Washington. Similarly to the work of Dr Ekman in Chapter 21 (page 50), Gottman reads and scores every conceivable emotion that a married couple might express during conversation. Using this data, he can predict with 95% accuracy whether the marriage will survive over the long term – and the analysis can be made within 3 minutes of observation!

Obviously there is a huge range of possible emotions that can be expressed and some of those emotions are 'micro expressions' that flash past so quickly that the untrained eye would easily miss them. You could read Gottman's book *The Mathematics of Divorce*, though your partner might get a tad suspicious when you scrutinise their every facial expression over steak and chips!

An easier solution would be the 'Four Horsemen' method. Gottman believes you can find out all you need to know about the health of a relationship by focusing on what he calls the Four Horsemen – presumably because they foretell of marital apocalypse. They are: defensiveness, stonewalling, criticism and contempt. And it's contempt that's the flashing neon sign! If one or both partners show contempt towards the other, this is the single most important signal of impending doom.

The presence of contempt in a marriage is so toxic that it can even predict the physical health of the couple. Having someone you love express contempt towards you is apparently so stressful that it will ultimately affect your immune system. Gottman says, 'Contempt is special. If you can measure contempt, then all of a sudden you don't need to know every detail of the couple's relationship.'

Collier concludes his marriage guidance with, 'Nine times out of ten, the best thing that can happen to any young couple is to have to start out with little or nothing and work out their salvation together.' And no contempt either!

HERE'S AN IDEA FOR YOU...
If you want your marriage to last, take the time to discuss things that annoy you before your relationship degenerates into one of defensiveness, stony silence, criticism and contempt. This might not always be easy, but surely it's worth a try.

26 YOU DON'T NEED TO KNOW THE DETAIL

Collier urges us, *'Do not think that supply must come through one or two channels. It is not for you to dictate to Universal Mind the means through which It shall send Its gifts to you. There are millions of channels through which It can reach you.'* In other words, the 'how' is not your concern.

DEFINING IDEA...
Nobody succeeds beyond his or her wildest expectations unless he or she begins with some wild expectations.
~ RALPH CHARELL, AUTHOR

One of the major reasons why goal setting doesn't work for some people is that they become bogged down in the 'how'. This is especially true if the goal is a stretch – they want something quite different from their current experiences. What Collier reminds us, however, is that we don't need to worry about the 'how' – we just need to concern ourselves with the 'what'. If you do get entangled in the detail of how your desires might come about, you immediately close down those millions of channels through which they could reach you.

The 'how' is not important, what is important is that you, 'Plant the seed of desire. Nourish it with clear visualisation of the ripened fruit. Water it with sincere faith. But leave the means to Universal Mind... Open up your mind. Clear out the channels of thought. Keep yourself in a state of receptivity. Gain a mental attitude in which you are constantly expecting good.'

It is these positive expectations that are so critical to success. If you remember from Chapter 12 (page 32) some of the quirks of quantum physics... when looking at the tiniest building blocks of life, scientists were astounded to discover that the particles behave differently depending on what the scientists observing them expected! It's the same in your life – we will rise or fall to meet our expectations or those others have of us.

No doubt you will have heard of the self-fulfilling prophecy, but do you know who first coined the term? It was a sociologist called Robert K. Merton. In his book, *Social Theory and Social Structure*, he states, 'The self-fulfilling prophecy is, in the beginning a false definite of the situation evoking a new behaviour which makes the original false conception come "true". This specious validity of the self-fulfilling prophecy perpetuates a reign of error. For the prophet will cite the actual course of events as proof that he was right from the very beginning.'

In other words, if you make up your mind about something then you immediately influence your behaviour and ultimately, your results. Whether your assumption is true or not is irrelevant because the belief that it is will alter your behaviour to bring about a 'reign of error' that vindicates your initial assumption.

So, forget about the 'how'... Collier reminds us, 'your part is to impress upon Mind your need, your earnest desire, your boundless belief in the resources and the willingness of Universal Mind to help you.' In other words, expect the best and it will do the rest!

HERE'S AN IDEA FOR YOU...
If you have children, they will rise or fall to meet your expectations of them. Believe in them, encourage them and they will learn to believe in themselves. Armed with this, the greatest of all parental gifts, there is no end to what they might achieve.

27 THE IMPORTANCE OF PERCEPTION

Collier says, *'It is absolutely necessary for every man to believe in himself, before he can make the most of himself. All of us have something to sell. It may be our goods, it may be our abilities, it may be our services.'* **Perception is everything, especially in business.**

DEFINING IDEA...
The image is more than an idea. It is a vortex or cluster of fused ideas and is endowed with energy.
~ EZRA POUND, US POET

Business is all about perception, yet so many businesses really get it wrong. For example, how many websites have you visited that scream 'amateur!' with every flashing, aqua marine pixel on the page? Also, business brochures that look like a high school project attempting to convince the reader of 'state-of-the-art technilojical advances'. OK, maybe the spelling error isn't that obvious, but you know what I mean. Foolish spelling mistakes and flashing smiley faces can be devastating for business development!

Business is all about trust and everything you do in your own business will build or diminish that trust. Everything from the way your staff answer the phone to the letterhead, website and business cards comes together to create a perception that either inspires a sale – or doesn't.

In a crowded and competitive market it's often difficult to stand out and create the right impression. When I'm not writing books such as this, I am a ghost-writer, specialising in non-fiction books for busy professionals, entrepreneurs and international speakers. Time and again, I've seen how being an 'author' transforms perception and it's no coincidence that an author is immediately assumed to be an 'author-ity'.

In 2006, my own experiences were confirmed by RainToday.com and Wellesley Hills Group when they published a report entitled *The Business Impact of Writing a Book*. Based on an extensive study of business book authors, an impressive 96% of authors reported that publishing a book positively influenced their business. The book improved their brand, generated more speaking engagements, and generated more clients, better clients and more leads. Authors were able to charge higher fees as demand for their services rose and the book allowed the business to close more deals. The overwhelming outcome of this research was, 'Assuming you have something worthwhile to say in a book, write one!'

I've since written a tome to help people do just that – *How to Write a Book in 33 Days… Develop your Brand, Establish yourself as an Expert, Protect your IP and Make More Money Without the Struggle*. You can find it on my website (www.wordarchitect.com), if you want to know more.

Perception is just a door opener. Presenting a professional, competent image to would-be clients and customers is the first step, but you must be able to back this up with impeccable service and quality. A good first impression, but poor delivery is ultimately just as damaging. So, if you happen to screw up, Collier suggests, 'You've got to feel the same personal solicitude over a customer lost, as a revivalist over a backslider, and hold special services to bring him back into the fold.'

HERE'S AN IDEA FOR YOU…

If you are self employed or run a business, take another look at your marketing collaterals. Ask yourself if they truly present the sort of professional image that you seek. If not, take action to rectify this, especially when it comes to your website.

28 BE OPTIMISTIC

In *The Secret of the Ages*, Collier tells us, 'A happy disposition is the result – not the cause – of happy, cheery thinking. Health and prosperity are the results primarily of optimistic thoughts. You make the pattern. You will never cultivate a brave, courageous demeanour by thinking cowardly thoughts. You cannot gather figs from thistles.'

DEFINING IDEA...
Optimism is an intellectual choice.
~ DIANE SCHNEIDER, PHOTOGRAPHER

Until recently, the field of psychology has been largely focused on the negative, treating mental illness rather helping to facilitate mental well-being. If you are in any doubt about this, try telling a group of friends that you are going to a psychiatrist and note their concern and furtive glances towards one another.

Thankfully one man who has done a great deal to rectify this imbalance is US psychologist Dr Martin Seligman. Seligman is perhaps most famous for his work on learned helplessness.

When it comes to the glass and whether it's half-full or half-empty, it's complicated. Some people are just born with a more optimistic outlook and it's simply part of their instinctive nature. For them, being optimistic is easy. Then there are the natural pessimists for whom encouragement to be optimistic is akin to asking them to grow a third arm!

But pessimism and optimism are also the result of nurture and what's learned can be unlearned too. What Seligman discovered was that outlook is also down to conditioning. Remember Hebbian learning from Chapter 23 (page

54)? If you react in the same way over time, the neural connection becomes stronger and transforms into a mental habit, resulting in more of the same. With negativity, eventually that pessimism manifests itself as depression. We effectively learn to behave helplessly in a given situation, usually after experiencing an inability to escape that situation. The conditioning becomes so strong that even when that person could change the unpleasantness of harmless circumstances, they won't choose to do so. This was a situation that Seligman had seen time and again in severely depressed patients. He argued, therefore, that depression and related mental illness was in part the result of the perceived absence of control.

The optimism that Seligman talks of is not some naive Pollyannaish 'positive thinking' optimism, rather an expression of what he calls 'explanatory style'. Dr Seligman found that optimists didn't take negative events personally – a missed train or a failed exam was isolated to a particular incident and nothing more than a temporary setback, which could be overcome with effort. On the other hand, a pessimist viewed such events as their fault – evidence of a broader malaise, which would plague them forever and couldn't be fixed, regardless of effort.

As Collier says, 'Just bear in mind that your real environment is within you. All the factors of success or failure are in your inner world. You make that inner world – and through it your outer world.' Everything can be changed just by our attitude and willingness to take the ups and downs of life a little less personally.

HERE'S AN IDEA FOR YOU...

Next time something negative happens, remember you have a choice: you can take it personally and make yourself feel extra-bad about the situation or see it as an invitation to do things differently so that you don't keep on repeating the same error. One route gives you choice, the other makes you depressed.

29 GOOD NEWS FOR COUCH POTATOES

Collier states, 'In this day of the gymnasium and the daily dozen, it may sound impractical to suggest that it is the mind, not the body, which needs the care. But I am far from the first to suggest it.' Apparently one successful London physician also suggested yawning and stretching were sufficient!

On the face of it, this sounds like excellent news. The idea that I don't have to visit the gym and our dog could walk herself is extremely appealing, especially when I have deadlines to meet.

DEFINING IDEA...
Ill-health, of body or of mind, is defeat. Health alone is victory. Let all men, if they can manage it, contrive to be healthy.
~ THOMAS CARLYLE, SCOTTISH WRITER

The fact that the body still operates remarkably well regardless of what we do to it can be seen on the bizarre TV show *Freaky Eaters*. In the show, a nutritionist and much-needed psychologist try to wean grown adults off extremely limited and unhealthy diets. For example, there was Adrian England, who lived on spaghetti hoops, toast, crisps, chips, sweets and fizzy drinks – and nothing else. Now I'm as partial to spaghetti hoops as the next person, but I'm not sure even Mr Collier's physician friend would think this was a good idea!

Joanne Adams from Middlesbrough never made the transition from mushy food to solids as a child. Consequently, at 19 years old, her diet consisted of mashed potatoes! If she was feeling a little frisky and fancied a change, she'd roast, chip or even crisp her potatoes! Kevin Johnson travelled internationally for business, but survived on salt and vinegar crisps and cheese and tomato pizza. Let's hope he didn't travel to anywhere exotic, where refusing food is a sign of disrespect… 'Would you join us for some sheep's eyes?' 'Mmm, you don't have a cheese and tomato pizza instead, by any chance?'

And finally, lecturer Pete Turner who had a long-standing fear of vegetables that meant he ate far more meat than perhaps was good for him. As well as dietary problems, he was also having relationship issues because his girlfriend Beth was a strict vegetarian!

The amazing thing about all these people was that they were able to function. If food is the body's fuel, it's a miracle that they could get out of bed in the morning. And yet they did and many were successful in other areas of their lives and this makes me wonder about Collier's theory.

Collier said, 'You can get the same results without the physical exercise by visualizing in your mind's eye the figure of the man you want to be, by intensely desiring it, by BELIEVING that you have it.'

I've always found it deeply unfair that you don't burn calories through thinking, reading or learning. Perhaps, in a hundred years, we will know enough about the human body to understand that keeping it healthy and strong is just a matter for the mind, but until then I think we will all have to take a little more responsibility for our personal well-being.

HERE'S AN IDEA FOR YOU…

Unless you have mastered the art of imagining yourself healthy while sitting on the couch watching Dr Phil, you are going to have to vacate said couch and do something. Just twenty minutes of light activity each day can make all the difference.

30 THE LAW OF ATTRACTION

Collier asks, *'Look around you. What businesses are going ahead? What men are making the big successes? Are they the ones who grab the passing dollar, careless of what they offer in return? Or is it those who are striving always to give a little greater value, a little more work, than they are paid for?'*

Collier goes on to talk about reciprocity, although he doesn't refer to it as such. Reciprocity is the innate drive for us to return favours or balance the books in response to a gift or favour. It is this potent force that is activated when you go that extra mile.

DEFINING IDEA...
Always render more and better service than is expected of you, no matter what your task may be.
~ OG MANDINO, SPEAKER AND AUTHOR

'When scales are balanced evenly, a trifle of extra weight thrown into either side overbalances the other effectively as a ton.' This is why being an author has such kudos. If you are pitching for new business and there's an even match between you and your competitors, having your own book can be enough to tip the balance in your favour.

Going the extra mile will always differentiate you and your business from the competition – 'a little better value, a little extra effort, makes the man or the business stand out from the great mass of mediocrity like a tall man among pygmies, and brings results out of all proportion to the additional effort involved'.

What's really fascinating about reciprocity is that it works, regardless of whether or not you like the person who has done you the favour! In April

2005, Iceland voted overwhelmingly to grant citizenship to former world chess champion Bobby Fischer. At the time, he was a fugitive from US law enforcement, publicly supported the September 11 hijackers and had broken UN sanctions by playing a chess game in the former Yugoslavia. The reason for this strange move on Iceland's part was because Fischer had done them a big favour, 33 years previously!

In 1972, Fischer was due to challenge Russian master Boris Spassky in what was dubbed the Chess Match of the Century, which was to be played in Iceland. The controversy surrounding Fischer and his demands made front-page news around the world as it was unclear whether he would even show up for the match. But he did and, as one Icelandic reporter put it, Fischer, 'put Iceland on the international map'. The country's willingness to grant Fischer citizenship when no one else would have him allowed Iceland to return the favour, even though many disliked him.

Collier reminds us that, 'It pays – not merely altruistically, but in good, hard round dollars – to give a little more value than seems necessary, to work a bit harder than you are paid for. It's that extra ounce of value that counts. The law of attraction is service. We receive in proportion as we give out.' But for the record, it's better to be likeable too!

HERE'S AN IDEA FOR YOU...

Help others if you can. If you are in business and can assist someone, even if you won't get paid for that assistance, then do so. Don't always look for payment or what you might receive in return.

31 MAKE THE WORLD BETTER

Collier says, *'You don't have to retire to a cell and pray. That is a selfish method – selfish concern for your own soul to the exclusion of all others... You've got to DO something, to USE the talents God has given you to make the world better for your having been in it.'*

DEFINING IDEA...
Everyone according to their talent and every talent according to its work.
~ FRENCH PROVERB

In her book *Sacred Contracts*, Caroline Myss talks about the idea of being on this earth to fulfil a sacred agreement. She says, 'By coming to know your mission, you can live your life in a way that makes best use of your energy. When you are working well with your energy, you are also making the best expression of your personal power. I call this living in accord with your Sacred Contract.'

The challenge, however, is that most of us don't know what that is. And often the personal development industry, which has flourished to assist in that quest, has done more harm than good. We are told 'anything's possible' and that we can all do whatever we want to do – if we just put our mind to it. But this misses the point... Why would you want to struggle to squash your square peg into a round hole? Wouldn't it just be easier and more productive to find a round one?

The sacred contract or innate talent that you have does not necessarily predispose you to a particular profession or niche; it's not that precise. Besides, we can't all be rock guitar gods, film stars or sporting heroes, but we can all be happy if we understand our innate operating system and learn to work with, instead of against it.

The ID System®, a profiling technique based on instinct, not behaviour and developed by Paul Burgess, is incredibly helpful in uncovering your innate operating system. I learned about Instinctive Drives when I worked with Paul on his book and was extremely impressed with its accuracy and application. It is made up of four drives – Verify, Authenticate, Complete and Improvise. You can be driven towards or away from each drive or be neutral. What makes it so useful is that unlike so many profiling techniques, it doesn't focus on *what* you do but *why* you do what you do. And the difference is extremely important if you are to uncover your innate gifts and talents.

The ID System allows you to understand your natural strengths and vulnerabilities so you can seek out professions that capitalise on those strengths and minimise the vulnerabilities. If you know what drives you – deadlines, pressure, maintaining order, routine, minimising risk, creating things, thinking about things, etc., then you can match that operating style to any number of professional or personal situations.

Collier tells us that if we use our talents – whatever they are – to the very best of our abilities and seek to improve and build upon them: 'It matters not how small your service – using it will make it greater.'

HERE'S AN IDEA FOR YOU...

If you don't know what you want to do when you 'grow up' and you're forty-five, don't panic! Try taking the ID questionnaire (www.idcentral.com.au) and first see what makes you happiest and most effective. This will help illuminate the path towards your sacred contract.

32 KARMIC JUSTICE WILL PREVAIL

Collier agrees with the statement, *'Summed up, the result of all my experiences, pleasant and unpleasant, is that man gets back exactly what he gives out, only multiplied.'* So, whatever you dish out, you will yourself experience – only amplified. It's karmic justice.

Collier says, 'Theosophists call it the law of karma; humanitarians call it the law of Service; businessmen call it the law of common sense; some call it the law of love.'

DEFINING IDEA...
What goes around, comes around.
~ PROVERB

Physician and author Deepak Chopra refers to karma as one of the seven spiritual laws of success adding, 'Every action generates a force of energy that returns to us in like kind… what we sow is what we reap. And when we choose actions that bring happiness and success to others, the fruit of our karma is happiness and success.'

Miceal Ledwith puts it this way, 'The really enlightened person will see that every action has a reaction with which I must deal, and if I'm wise, I am not going to do stuff that will cause me to have to face it and resolve it and balance it in my soul later… we'll have to learn that sooner or later.' Ledwith's comments are all the more profound because he was ordained as a Catholic priest in 1967. He is also a lecturer in theology and between 1980 and 1997, served three terms as a member of the international Theological Commission, a small group who advise on theological matters referred to them by the Pope or the Congregation for the Doctrine of Faith.

Heaven and hell are therefore not potential destinations based on past performance, they are earthly karmic experiences based on our thoughts and actions. If you are morally bankrupt and think nothing of hurting others, if you steal or are addicted to substances that destroy your life, if you look for difference and are filled with hate and intolerance, then no one needs to judge you and send you to Hell – you are already living there. And that's karmic justice.

If you do the best you can with the resources you have, if you seek to find the good in others and work hard to support yourself and your loved ones, if you look for joy and love and laugh often, then no one is judging you – you are already living in heaven. And that too is karmic justice. You create your own world by the thoughts you have and the actions (or inactions) that spring from those thoughts. It's that simple.

I totally agree with Collier when he says, '[Karma] is not true because I say so, nor because anybody else says so; it is just true.' The law of karma says that no debt in the universe goes unpaid. Certainly, I have found it irritatingly active in my life and have also seen it operate with awe-inspiring precision in others.

HERE'S AN IDEA FOR YOU...

You are a product of your choices, conscious and unconscious. Before you do anything, ask yourself, 'Would I like to experience what I am about to do?' Karmic justice says you will do so – make sure you choose wisely.

33 THE DISCOURAGEMENT DISEASE

Collier tells of the time when the Devil had a sale, offering all the tools of his trade. Hatred, malice, envy, despair and sickness were all there. Most expensive of all was a wedge named *'discouragement'* and when the Devil was asked why, he explained, *'Because I can use this one so much more easily than the others.'*

No one knew that discouragement belonged to the Devil, 'with it I can open doors that are tight bolted against the others. Once I get inside I can use any tool that suits me best.'

> DEFINING IDEA...
> *Most of our pocket wisdom is conceived for the use of the mediocre people, to discourage them from ambitious attempts, and generally console them in their mediocrity.*
> ~ ROBERT LOUIS STEVENSON, SCOTTISH WRITER

Sadly, it is often those who love us most who are the most discouraging. Sometimes this occurs out of self-interest – if you do well where they failed, they will feel even worse about themselves than they may do already and that's not an appealing prospect.

The other reason why those we love discourage us is because they are trying to protect us from the big bad world. Perhaps, years before, they tried to pursue a dream and it didn't end well; that hurt is still present and they genuinely don't want you, their loved one, to go through that same pain and so they discourage your efforts to change.

There is a story often told in personal development seminars about an experiment that involved monkeys in an enclosure. A bunch of bananas was placed on a high platform and it wasn't long before the monkeys spotted the fruit and went to retrieve it... Only when they tried they were blasted with a jet of cold water. It didn't hurt the monkeys, but it wasn't pleasant either. After several attempts and corresponding soakings, the monkeys stopped trying. One by one, the original monkeys were replaced by a new monkey and every time the new monkey would attempt to go for the bananas the rest of the monkeys would stop him, even though the water jet was no longer in the enclosure. It got to a point where none of the original monkeys were in the enclosure and yet not one of them attempted to retrieve the fresh juicy bananas placed on the platform.

I've searched for a reference to this experiment and can't find it, so this might just be an urban myth, but the message remains correct. In parts of Asia, elephants are trained by discouragement: a rope is tied round a baby elephant's leg and he is tethered to a tree. Struggle as he might, he can't free himself but then he grows up and he's more than capable of ripping the tree from its roots. However, his early discouragement is enough to keep him trapped by nothing more than a length of rope attached to his leg.

Collier reminds us that, 'no one knows how small is the margin between failure and success. Frequently the two are separated only by the width of that one word – discouragement.'

HERE'S AN IDEA FOR YOU...

Keep all your discouraging thoughts to yourself. Regardless of what people you love tell you about their plans, back them up. And if you can't do that, just keep quiet!

34 THINGS YOU CAN CONTROL VS THE THINGS YOU CAN'T

Collier states, *'You have a right to dominion over all things – over your body, your environment, your business, your health. Develop these requisites and you will gain that dominion.'* That is done by mastering and directing our thoughts in a constructive way.

DEFINING IDEA...
While we may not be able to control all that happens to us, we can control what happens inside us.
~ BENJAMIN FRANKLIN, US FOUNDING FATHER

The world is split in two – the things you can control and those you can't control. Most of us spend an inordinate amount of time stressing about things we can't control. If we were to direct the same or even half of our energy focusing on the things we could change, then we might be surprised how unimportant the rest becomes.

To help with this, you need to master the art of non-engagement. The idea was first presented to me by business productivity consultant and author Brendan Nichols, who refers to the principle of non-engagement as one of the seven deadly sins of time and says, 'This isn't about being heartless, it's about head space. If something is bothering you, fix it and move on. Don't let your focus and attention be robbed by something that you can't change.'

And in case you are wondering, 'other people' don't fall into the category of things you can change. The great Gandhi once said, 'for things to change, I must change'. You must become accustomed to seeing your world as a learning experience that mirrors back to you aspects of your nature that may need adjusting so you can evolve into a better person.

The spiritual idea is that your external world is merely a reflection of your internal world. So, for example if someone is upsetting you, then it's very likely that you are seeing a part of yourself. This situation has arisen to give you the opportunity to see yourself in action, discover what it feels like to be on the receiving end of your own behaviour and so make the necessary changes. Often we meet people in life who force us to examine our own behaviour and in so doing offer us the opportunity to change and grow.

Remember Pete Turner (page 67) who was terrified of vegetables? Do you think it was just ironic that his girlfriend was a strict vegetarian or that his subconscious chose his vegetarian lover so that he would be forced to face his fears and fix his diet before he did himself permanent damage? Often we do much more for people we love than we will ever do for ourselves.

Collier urges us to remember that, 'you are a part of Universal Mind and that the part shares every property of the whole'. In other words, it is impossible for us to see something that is not also part of us. Or as the ancient spiritual text of the Talmud states, 'We do not see things as they are – we see them as we are'.

HERE'S AN IDEA FOR YOU...

Is someone really annoying you right now? Try to discern a personality trait or characteristic that is pushing your buttons. Have you ever behaved in that way to another person? If so, view the situation as an invitation to change.

35 FEAR IS CREATIVE THOUGHT IN NEGATIVE FORM

Colliers asks, *'Has that old witch – bad luck – ever camped on your doorstep? Have ill health, misfortune and worry ever seemed to dog your footsteps? If so, you will be interested in knowing that YOU were the procuring cause of all that trouble. For fear is merely creative thought in negative form.'*

DEFINING IDEA...

Half of the American people have never read a newspaper. Half have never voted for a President. One hopes it is the same half.

~ GORE VIDAL, US WRITER AND POLITICIAN

Interestingly, Collier refers back to the 1920s when, at the beginning of the decade, the business outlook was fine, 'everything looked rosy and life flowed along like a song. We had crops worth ten billions of dollars. We had splendid utilities, great railways, almost unlimited factory capacity. Everyone was busy. The government had a billion dollars in actual money. The banks were sound. The people were well employed. Wages were good. Prosperity was general. Then something happened. A wave of fear swept over the country.' He was, of course, talking about the advent of the Great Depression.

Fast forward eight decades and it would appear that our karmic lessons have not been learned at all. After years of record profits and eye-watering bonuses, the financial industry discovered it wasn't prudent after all to lend money to subprime lenders or people who had no way or inclination of paying it back. However, the debt had long since been packaged up into acceptable, risk assessed investment opportunities, which started to sour on a major scale. Banks panicked and jammed on the lending brakes, and it is the resulting credit crunch that has made an already disastrous situation ten times worse.

As Niall Ferguson wrote in his book, *The Ascent of Money*, 'The subprime butterfly had flapped its wings and triggered a global hurricane.' That hurricane still rages on and, according to the International Monetary Fund (IMF), the subprime mortgage collapse is likely to cost the world economy a staggering $945 billion!

As of August 2009 the UK had officially been in recession for 15 months. In June 2009, the Public Sector Net Debt stood at a jaw-dropping £799 billion – equivalent to £32,000 per household! The UK government is currently paying £76 million a day to service that debt! Meanwhile, unemployment is at a 14-year high.

Collier ends with a statement that rings as true for the financial disasters of the Great Depression as the most recent one, ''Tis true that readjustments were necessary. 'Tis true that prices were too high, that inventories were too big, that values generally were inflated. But it wasn't necessary to burst the balloon to let out the gas. There are orderly natural processes of readjustment that bring things to their proper level with the least harm to anyone. But fear and panic knows no reason.'

Fear and greed can build and destroy in equal measure. Let's hope that when we finally get out of this mess, the lessons learned will have been painful enough for us *not* to repeat them in another one hundred years!

HERE'S AN IDEA FOR YOU...

Vote! Rocks and hard places may spring to mind, but governments should never get to power because of the silent majority. If you don't like the way your country is being run, then register your dissatisfaction or keep quiet!

36 MIND OVER MATTER

Collier suggests, *'Your body is just like clay in the hands of a potter. Your mind can make of it what it will. The clay has nothing to say about what form it shall take. Neither have your head, your heart, your lungs, your digestive organs anything to say about how conditions shall affect them.'*

The big problem with this idea is that while it may be true, and certainly there is plenty of evidence to back it up, we are still no further forward in working out why.

The power of the mind over the body may be seen in the healing power of placebo medicine. How is it possible that distilled water, sugar pills and even mock surgery heals patients of serious and potentially fatal diseases when all conventional treatment has failed?

DEFINING IDEA...
I have learned to use the word impossible with the greatest caution.
– WERNHER VON BRAUN, GERMAN-AMERICAN PHYSICIST

According to Deepak Chopra, in his book *Quantum Healing*, the skeleton is fully replaced every three months. Your skin is replaced each month, your stomach lining every four days and your liver every 6 weeks. In fact, 98% of the atoms in your body today were not there a year ago. So, if this constant regeneration takes place as cells die off and are replaced, why do people remain sick? If the body is just like clay, what influences the hands of the potter? More importantly, why does the potter recreate the diseased tissue rather than create new perfect tissue?

And here's the billion-dollar question... There is no doubt that the mind can, and does play a huge role in the body. In my own life I've seen this most dramatically when I did a 15-m (50-ft) fire walk without a single blister. Those who were not mentally prepared did burn, so this is not a parlour trick. At the other end of the spectrum of evidence are people with extraordinary control over their mind-body connection, who are instantly able to manifest thought into material reality!

In *The Holographic Universe*, author Michael Talbot writes about Sathya Sai Baba, an Indian holy man living in a distant corner of southern India. According to many eyewitnesses, including psychologist Erlendur Haraldsson, who spent over 10 years studying him, Sai Baba could pluck lockets, rings and jewellery out of thin air. He also produced an endless supply of Indian delicacies and sweets and huge volumes of *vibuti* (sacred ash) would pour out of his hands. Granted, masses of ash would make a terrible mess of the front room, sacred or otherwise, but reports of this type are not unique and yet they pose more questions than they answer.

Collier tells us that our body doesn't 'decide whether [it] shall be dizzy or diseased or lame. It is mind that makes this decision.' Perhaps that is so, but despite the decades that have passed since he wrote his work, the mechanics of that process remain shrouded in mystery.

HERE'S AN IDEA FOR YOU...
If you are sceptical of the mind-body connection, go along to a weekend workshop that offers fire walking as a novel marketing trick. Even a few steps will burn if you look down or don't do the preliminary mental preparation.

37 FIRST MIND, THEN BODY

Collier says, *'You fear ill health, when if you concentrate that same amount of thought upon good health you would insure the very condition you fear to lose. Functional disturbances are caused solely by the mind through wrong thinking. The remedy for them is not a drug, but right thinking.'*

Seventeenth-century French philosopher Rene Descartes made a mistake when he said, 'There is nothing included in the concept of the body that belongs to the mind and nothing of the mind that belongs to the body.' This assertion split the two and so began the ongoing struggle to reunite mind and body in modern medicine.

> DEFINING IDEA...
> *Some patients I see are actually draining into their bodies the diseased thoughts of their minds.*
> ~ ZACHARY T. BERCOVITZ, US DOCTOR AND WRITER

Dr Carl Simonton is one of the many doctors dedicated to bringing the mind and body back together again. He says, 'The ways in which we respond to the stresses of life are habitual, dictated by our unconscious beliefs about who we are, who we "should" be and the way the world and other people are and should be. These patterns of behaviour form a total orientation or stance toward life.'

American psychotherapist Albert Ellis warned of the damage 'should' and 'must' create for us, adding, 'musterbation is evil and pernicious'. And there is growing evidence that the stance we adopt as a consequence of these internal pressures can have a direct impact on our health.

In the book, *Type A Behaviour and Your Heart*, Drs Meyer Friedman and Ray Rosenman wrote that the constantly pressured, highly competitive character associated with a Type A personality has a direct correlation to increased heart disease. According to Dr Carl Simonton, there are also many shared characteristics in those suffering from rheumatoid arthritis, stomach ulcers, asthma and cancer.

Writing nearly 2,000 years ago, the physician Galen observed that cheerful women were less prone to cancer than depressed ones! In 1846, Dr Walter Hyle Walshe stated, 'Much has been written on the influence of mental misery, sudden reversal of fortunes, and habitual gloominess of temper on the disposition of [cancer]. I have myself met with cases in which the connection appeared so clear that questioning its reality would have seemed a struggle against reason.' Sir James Paget also expressed his conviction that depression plays a vital role in the occurrence of cancer in his classic text, *Surgical Pathology*, published in 1870 – an observation truly frightening when you consider that in 2008, more than 164 million antidepressant prescriptions were written in the US alone.

Caroline Myss is a highly respected medical intuitive as well as bestselling author. After conducting over 8,000 readings, where she intuits medical challenges through the patient's energy field, Myss states, 'our biography becomes our biology… In other words, the little troubles and major traumas that we go through take up residence and live in our bodies and affect or block our energy.' According to Collier, the trouble is 'not in the organs, but in the mind'.

HERE'S AN IDEA FOR YOU…

Never mind what you should or must do. Do it or don't do it, but do stop stressing about it! If you are depressed, it's a sign that you need to change something, not take drugs.

38 TO FEAR OR NOT TO FEAR, THAT IS THE QUESTION

Collier says, *'The Bible contains one continuous entreaty to cast out fear. From beginning to end, the admonition "Fear not" is insistent.'* Yet a few short pages later he talks of the Old Testament and how war, pestilence, fire and flood are the common lot of mankind.

Fear, it would seem, takes sides and is religiously selective. 'Fear not' may indeed be the insistence of the Bible, but there is a very significant caveat. You can only 'fear not' if you believe in God, otherwise you are heading for hell in a hand basket!

> DEFINING IDEA...
> *In morals what begins in fear usually ends in wickedness; in religion what begins in fear usually ends in fanaticism. Fear, either as a principle or a motive, is the beginning of all evil.*
> ~ ANNA BROWNELL JAMESON, IRISH WRITER

What puzzles me is the contradictory nature of this idea and its ramifications in the modern world. If we know, for example, through decades of research and study that there is a distinct correlation between certain emotions and habitual feelings and the onset of disease, surely we should be doing all we can to diminish those feelings and emotions in our lives? Collier states very clearly that, 'Fear is the primary cause of all bodily impairment.'

If that's the case, surely religion is bad for your health? If we were to play the word association game and I said, 'Religion' and you named emotions that spring to mind, I can guess guilt, shame and fear would be on your list. Yet habitual guilt, shame or fear has been shown to be extremely damaging to one's health.

Besides, if you expect the worst from people all the time, aren't you more likely to get it? The Pygmalion Effect, named after George Bernard Shaw's play *Pygmalion* in which a professor makes a bet that he can teach a poor flower girl to behave like an upper-class lady, is the phenomenon whereby you get what you expect. So, if religion states everyone is born evil and must spend their life repenting, isn't this by default expecting the worst from everyone?

I have to say that I'm with Gore Vidal when he says, 'The great unmentionable evil at the center of our culture is monotheism. From a barbaric Bronze Age text known as the Old Testament, three anti-human religions have evolved – Judaism, Christianity, and Islam. These are sky-god religions. They are, literally, patriarchal – God is the Omnipotent Father – hence the loathing of women for 2,000 years in those countries afflicted by the sky-god and his earthly male delegates.'

As Collier so rightly states, 'If we would only try to realize that God is not some far-off Deity, not some stern judge, but the beneficent force that we recognize as Nature – the life Principle that makes the flowers bud and the plants grow.' And truly there is nothing to fear from that God. There is no need for fear, shame, guilt, remorse, depression, hate or intolerance.

HERE'S AN IDEA FOR YOU...
The easiest way to break a negative emotional state is to move physically. So, put on some loud music and dance in your living room or sing at the top of your voice.

39 UPS AND DOWNS OF LIFE

Collier reminds us, *'Struggle there is. And struggle there will always be. But struggle is merely wrestling with trial. We need difficulties to overcome. But there is nothing to be afraid of.'* His words remind us that life is full of ups and downs, but they should be relished, not feared.

> DEFINING IDEA...
> *Whatever the ups and downs of detail within our limited experience, the larger whole is primarily beautiful.*
> ~ GREGORY BATESON, UK ANTHROPOLOGIST

If you've ever been connected to an electrocardiograph machine (EKG or ECG) in hospital to measure your heartbeat, you will notice the ups and downs of the very thing keeping you alive. Across the screen, the line travels in a series of peaks and troughs, beeping intermittently to tell you that your heart is normal, that you are still alive. This is the beat of your life, of every life, and it goes through a series of spikes and dips in the same way as we travel from birth to death.

You need contrast to be able to appreciate the difference. Without black, we wouldn't appreciate white; without good, we wouldn't understand bad and without sadness, we wouldn't be grateful for happiness. Instead of looking at life as challenges to survive, we just need to appreciate that it is full of ups and downs.

Those ups and downs, by the way, are not events but emotional attachments and interpretations of events and circumstances. It is emotion that gives us the rollercoaster ride of being alive. Emotion allows us to survive as a species and to evolve over time. If there was no emotion our life would be bland and without it there would be no peaks and troughs, life would be monotonous and dull. Indeed, this is borne out by some patients who suffer a frontal lobe brain injury. Often they have no interest in activities and little response to sad or funny situations – the highs and lows are effectively extinguished.

Instead of fretting about ups and downs, try to regard them as trials to wrestle and opportunities to learn more about yourself and what you are capable of. See them as opportunities to evolve into a better person. A pearl is created because a grain of sand permanently irritates the oyster and it is forced to act, so the oyster coats the grain of sand over and over again until a beautiful precious pearl is made. Perhaps that's how we must learn to view the irritants in our life – as an opportunity to create a pearl of wisdom.

Pain and discomfort are invitations to change. They are not meant to be permanent situations, but encouraging prods towards a new direction. If you ignore these gentle reminders, eventually the universe will smack you round the head with a baseball bat. That's not to say that you should go looking for trouble but when it finds you, just deal with it and move on. Collier also suggests that you, 'Banish from among your associates any man with a negative outlook on life.'

HERE'S AN IDEA FOR YOU...
The twists and turns are just part of life, so get used to them! You may not be able to predict or plan for them, but you can always decide what to make those events indicate. Choose helpful meanings.

40 WIPE THE SLATE CLEAN

Collier asks, *'Do you know why old army men would rather have soldiers of 18 or 20 than mature men of 30 or 40? Not because they can march farther… [or] carry more. They can't! But because when they go to sleep at night, they really fall asleep. They wipe the slate clean!'*

Apparently, younger men wake refreshed and ready for a new world and a new day, but older ones carry the nervous strain of one day over to the next.

> DEFINING IDEA…
> *Look at life through the windshield, not the rear-view mirror.*
> ~ BYRD BAGGETT, US SPEAKER

The cynical among us might argue that old army men prefer young soldiers because they are full of bravado, ego and stupidity and have not yet experienced the horrors of war nor drawn the inevitable conclusion that war can never end war. But the ability to wipe the slate clean is an important one to master. Remember Dr Martin Seligman and his theory of learned helplessness (page 64)? Together with psychiatrist George Valliant and psychologist Christopher Peterson, Seligman studied 99 members of Harvard's graduating class of 1939–44. Following graduation, these army men were given physical examinations every five years and were interviewed about their war experiences on their return from World War II.

Those who were optimistic in college were healthier in later life than the pessimists were. Seligman said, 'The men's explanatory style at age 25 predicted their health at 65. Around age 45 the health of the pessimists started to deteriorate more quickly.'

It is this explanatory style that is so crucial in learning how to wipe the slate clean. Those who view life from a more pessimistic perspective tend to see events that don't go according to plan or outright failures as a personal and permanent black mark against them as individuals, where optimists regard them as isolated events that could give up clues to improved performance next time. Optimists therefore have a natural propensity to wipe the slate clean. However, we all have a degree of optimism and pessimism within us – if you naturally lean towards the half-empty approach to life, you just have to practise the art of slate-wiping a little more consciously.

If things go well, bank that positive experience in your 'Happy Memory bank' and call on it whenever you need a little boost of confidence. And if they don't go so well, assess for improvements, find out what you might do differently and how you could improve your performance. Now hit the reset button, wipe the slate clean and try again tomorrow – without looking back. Your past does not dictate your future… unless you allow it to do so.

Collier suggests this ability to carry forward worry also affects most men in business, 'They never wipe the slate clean! They worry! And they carry each day's worries over to the next, with the result that some day the burden becomes more than they can carry.'

HERE'S AN IDEA FOR YOU…
When something goes well for you, review the day's events and look for clues as to your success. Revel in the memory and enjoy it. If it doesn't go so well, search for clues to your failure. Take a mental note not to repeat the error and wipe the slate clean.

41 RELAX

As Collier rightly points out, *'You feed and nourish the body daily. But few people give any thought to nourishing that far more important part – the Mind. To begin with, relax! Stretch out comfortably, let go of every muscle, loosen every bit of tension, forget every thought. Relax mentally and physically.'*

DEFINING IDEA...
A cheerful frame of mind, reinforced by relaxation, which in itself banishes fatigue, is the medicine that puts all ghosts of fear on the run.
~ GEORGE M ADAMS, US POLITICIAN

From the short description of how the reader should go about relaxing, it's clear that Collier is familiar with the work of the American physician, Edmund Jacobsen. In the early 1920s, Jacobsen developed a stress management and relaxation technique known as Progressive Muscle Relaxation (PMR). He argued that anxiety is always accompanied by muscular tension and if we could relax that muscular tension, anxiety would simultaneously be reduced. Jacobsen said, 'An anxious mind cannot exist within a relaxed body.'

PMR is a simple two-stage process that requires you to deliberately tense and release muscle groups while noticing how the muscle feels when you stop tensing it and allow the tension to drain away. Success of the process hinges on gaining an awareness of the difference between tense and relaxed muscles so you can fully experience a state of relaxation. It has been used to great effect for insomnia and simply to help people chill out and is still widely used in physical therapies. Opposite is a common instruction for PMR. First, tense your muscle groups for a slow count of five and then count to ten as you relax. Breathe in as you tense and out as you relax.

1. Tense your left foot and ankle first. Relax and then tense your right foot and ankle. Relax.
2. Tense your left calf and lower leg. Relax and then tense your right calf and lower leg. Relax.
3. Tense your left upper leg and relax, then tense your right upper leg. Relax.
4. Tense your whole right leg. Relax. Now tense your whole left leg. Relax.
5. Tense your buttocks and relax.
6. Tense your abdomen and relax.
7. Tense your chest and back, and relax.
8. Tense your left shoulder and biceps. Relax. Tense your right shoulder and biceps and relax.
9. Tense your left forearm and fist and relax. Tense your right forearm and fist, relax.
10. Tense your left hand and fingers. Relax. Tense your right hand and fingers and relax.
11. Tense the whole of your left arm and hand. Relax, then tense the whole of your right arm and hand. Relax.
12. Tense your neck and jaw, and relax.
13. Tense your facial muscles and relax.

We spend thousands on a home that we barely spend time in or a car that we might drive for just a few hours each day, but we rarely take time to relax the mind and body. Collier encourages, 'So let us try, each day, to set apart a few minutes time to give the Mind a repast. Few people know how to relax entirely. Most of us are on a continual strain, and it is this strain that brings on physical disturbances – not any real work we do.'

HERE'S AN IDEA FOR YOU...
Search online for a video tutorial on how to do PMR (there are quite a few to choose from on YouTube). Alternatively, buy a PMR CD. Oh, and don't listen to it while driving!

42 LIFE WILL FIND A WAY

According to Collier, Dr Jacques Loeb of the Rockefeller Institute conducted a series of tests where, *'potted rose bushes are brought into a room and placed in front of a closed window. If the plants are allowed to dry out, the aphides [parasites], previously wingless, change to winged insects.'*

> DEFINING IDEA...
> *Hunger, love, pain, fear are some of those inner forces which rule the individual's instinct for self-preservation.*
> ~ ALBERT EINSTEIN, SCIENTIST AND INVENTOR

Jacques goes on to conclude that it was 'evident that these tiny insects found that the plants on which they had been thriving were dead, and that they could therefore secure nothing more to eat and drink from this source. The only method by which they could save themselves from starvation was to grow temporary wings and fly, which they did.'

When the chips are down, parasites at the bottom of the food chain grow wings, so what can human beings do in the same situation? I am always staggered at just how capable we can be when the need arises. Take Aren Ralston, for example...

In April 2003, Ralston entered Utah's Bluejohn Canyon. Despite being an experienced climber, he made the near-fatal mistake of not telling anyone that he was going and not taking a mobile phone with him.

During his expedition, a 363 kg (800 lb) boulder shifted, crushing his right hand and forearm, and pinning them against the canyon wall. For six days, he tried unsuccessfully to free himself until he ran out of water. Dehydrated and delirious, Ralston snapped his radius and ulna bones and used the blunt blade of a multipurpose tool to cut off his lower arm. After freeing himself, he was then forced to trek 12.8 km (8 miles) to his truck. Luckily, he met a family on holiday from Holland, who helped him to safety.

The other amazing story is that of Joe Simpson, who was the first to reach the summit of Siula Grande in the Peruvian Andes, along with Simon Yates. Unfortunately, on the descent, Simpson fell and severely broke his leg. Without provisions, they needed to quickly make the descent. Tied together by a 91 m (300 ft) rope, Yates lowered Simpson down the mountain. However, disaster struck again and Yates was forced to cut the rope or they would both die. Simpson dropped 30 m (100 ft). Miraculously, he survived and spent three days crawling back to base camp. His survival is considered one of the greatest in mountaineering history.

Perhaps the superhuman force that I talked about in Chapter 2 (page 12) is our survival instinct. I really believe something miraculous occurs when the chips are down, but you cannot manufacture that predicament or call on it until you *really* need it. And if that is true, surely this raises very real questions about the validity of the welfare state. Does our desire to dish out endless benefits without assessing true need actually hinder folk from tapping into the 'Universal Supply' so they too can furnish themselves with temporary wings for migration to a better life?

HERE'S AN IDEA FOR YOU...

If these stories of survival against huge odds indicate some sort of cosmic safety net, what would you do in your life if you were sure that you would be forever protected from the worse case scenario?

43 THOUGHT IS THE DIRECTION, EMOTION IS THE FUEL

Collier says, *'Visualise the conditions you would like to see. Every time you do this, you impress the thought upon your subconscious mind. And the moment you can convince your subconscious mind of the truth of it – that moment your mind will proceed to make it true.'*

DEFINING IDEA...

Emotions are the chemistry to reinforce an experience neurologically. We remember things that are more heightened and more emotional, and that's the way it should be.

~ JOE DISPENZA, BIOCHEMIST, CHIROPRACTOR AND AUTHOR

It is emotion that allows your desires to be impressed on your subconscious mind. Unless you are a highly skilled shaman, such as those mentioned in Chapter 36 (page 81), you needn't worry that every passing fancy and stray thought that you have will be miraculously transferred into the material world. The subconscious mind is only interested in highly emotional thoughts; it uses emotion as a barometer of importance.

If you think back, you probably don't remember that much about your life. Chances are, you will only recall the really great and the really bad. Those experiences sear themselves into memory and play a pivotal role in learning and conditioned responses. It is the emotion in those events that causes the impact and if that is true for memory, then it's also true when you wish to create your future too.

Each emotion has a chemical signature in the body: a chain of amino acids made up of proteins is created in the hypothalamus for every type of emotion.

It is the absorption of that chemical cocktail by the cells in our body that gives rise to the feeling of that emotion. Emotion, therefore, is a two-way system, or as Elmer and Alyce Green, pioneers in the field of biofeedback, state: 'every change in the physiological state is accompanied by an appropriate change in the mental emotional state, conscious or unconscious, and conversely, every change in the mental emotional state, conscious or unconscious, is accompanied by an appropriate change in the physiological state'. Or, as Dr Carl Simonton puts it, 'mind, body and emotions are a unitary system – affect one and you affect the others'.

And as a freaky little reminder as to just how connected emotions, mind and body can be, consider the experiments conducted by the US Army Intelligence and Security Command in 1993. White blood cells scraped from the mouths of volunteers were centrifuged and placed in a test tube and then a lie detector probe was placed inside. The donor of the cells was then asked to watch TV with some violent scenes. When violence was depicted on the screen, the probe registered extreme excitation of the cells even though both cells and donor were in separate rooms – even when donor and cells were separated 50 miles the experiment could be successfully repeated!

Collier reminds us, 'Your mind is part of Universal Mind. And Universal Mind has all supply. You are entitled to, and you can have, just as much of that supply as you are able to appropriate. To expect less is to get less, for it dwarfs your power of receiving.'

HERE'S AN IDEA FOR YOU...

Remember Napoleon Hill's advice in Think and Grow Rich: *'All thoughts which have been emotionalized [given feeling] and mixed with faith begin immediately to translate themselves into their physical equivalent or counterpart.' And be grateful!*

44 THE TIME IS NOW

As a reminder against procrastination, Collier tells how, *'A Genii sent [a maiden] into a field of grain, promising her a rare gift if she would pick for him the largest and ripest ear she could find; His gift to be in proportion to the size and perfection of the ear.'*

There was only one condition – she must pluck just one ear and she couldn't backtrack. Thinking the task easy, she sees large, perfect ears of corn but is convinced there will be better ahead and so she leaves them, only to pass the most fertile soil. In the end, 'she found herself at the end of the field – empty handed as when she set out!'

> DEFINING IDEA...
> *We must not discriminate between things. Where things are concerned, there are no class distinctions. We must pick out what is good for us where we can find it.*
> ~ PABLO PICASSO, ARTIST AND SCULPTOR

Collier draws the apt correlation, 'So it is with life.' Instead of seizing opportunities as they arise, we assume something better is around the corner or that a more appropriate or perfect time will present itself down the road. As a result, we don't take the required leap of faith to start a new business or retrain for a profession that we long to be part of. We justify that procrastination by telling ourselves that we'll do it when we have more money in the bank, or the mortgage is paid off or the kids have left home. The lucky ones have change thrust upon them through redundancy, but the unlucky ones reach retirement worn out and exhausted from years of doing something they didn't enjoy, wondering where all the years went.

The other major life event being put on hold is parenthood. I do think it's slightly unfair how women such as me are viewed as cold, selfish and ladder climbing career bitches when in truth, most of us don't have children because we never met a man we wanted to have coffee with, never mind a child! If, or when we eventually do so, eggs and energy both are on the decline. Although apparently there are studies indicating that having children doesn't make you very happy, so perhaps what I perceive as pity and contempt is actually envy! It's a hypothesis backed up by the number of parents who seem to resonate with the TV advertisement for Wall's sausages in which a newborn is shown in his father's arms. It then cuts to the day when the boy leaves home with the message... we only select the two best bits!

Collier reminds us that, 'Every day offers its chance for happiness. But those rewards seem so small, those chances so petty, compared with the big things we see ahead. So we pass them by, never recognizing that the great position we look forward to, the shining prize we see in the distance, is just the sum of all the little tasks, the heaped-up result of all the little prizes that we must win as we go along.'

HERE'S AN IDEA FOR YOU...

Jungian psychologist James Hillman once said, 'You have to give up the life you have to get to the life that's waiting for you.' So, what do you have to give up to get what you want?

45 IT'S THE INVISIBLE THINGS THAT REALLY MATTER

Collier reminds us, *'The greatest powers of Nature are invisible. Love is invisible, but what greater power is there in life? Joy is invisible, happiness, peace and contentment. The radio is invisible – yet you hear it. It is the product of the law governing sound waves.'*

Much of what makes us human is invisible. Intuition is invisible, yet its existence is hard to ignore. Remember the art fake in Chapter 5 (page 18)? Some experts just knew it was a fake as soon as they looked at it, even though they were unable to explain why.

DEFINING IDEA...

Ninety-nine percent of who you are is invisible and untouchable.
– R. BUCKMINSTER FULLER, US VISIONARY AND AUTHOR

As the name suggests, these snap judgements are extremely fast, with no thought or logic involved. Part of this phenomenon is of course based on survival, but clearly there is something more. Perhaps these moments occur when we somehow reach through the veil of consciousness into the storehouse of universal or collective consciousness, giving us momentary access to higher wisdom.

Remember Simon Yates from Chapter 42 (page 93). Despite only ever having full support from Joe Simpson, Yates took a lot of heat for his decision to cut the rope. He was accused of saving himself, but the truth is if he hadn't cut the rope then both climbers would probably have died. Cutting the rope freed Yates to seek shelter while also dropping Simpson (albeit a long way!) to a sheltered spot. Had the two fallen while roped together, Simpson might still have survived, but Yates would have died. Had Yates not got to camp before Simpson eventually crawled in, almost certainly their travelling companion Richard Hawking would have left, giving both up for dead. Without anyone to help, Simpson would have died out in the mountains. By cutting the rope, therefore, Yates saved them both. Perhaps in that moment of truth he was able to reach through the veil and trust his difficult decision was the right one.

Billionaire investor George Soros' son has said, 'My father will sit down and give you theories to explain why he does this and that, but I remember seeing it as a kid. At least half of it is bull… the reason he changes his position is because his back starts killing him. He literally goes into spasm, and it's this early warning sign.' Clearly, Soros is a very smart guy, not least because he doesn't inform his shareholders that his investment strategy is based on back spasms! Perhaps if he did they might have him committed, and so he gives them what they need to hear to feel confident! We demand explanations, yet sometimes there just aren't any – at least none that are logical or comprehensible!

Perhaps we all have to learn to trust our intuition, knowing a little more. Otherwise we risk missing the magic! Collier asks, 'Because this Power of Universal Mind is invisible, is that any reason to doubt it?'

HERE'S AN IDEA FOR YOU...

If the things that are not important are only important when the things that are important are not (think about it!) and those things are invisible, why bend over backwards to struggle for extra trinkets when everything that really matters is invisible and you can't buy it?

46 ASSUME A VIRTUE

Collier says, *'You have only to keep in mind the experiences you wish to meet in order to control your own future... Shakespeare expresses the same thought in another way – "Assume a virtue if you have it not". Look the part. Dress the part. Act the part. Be successful in your own thoughts first.'*

DEFINING IDEA...
If you want a quality, act as if you already had it. Try the 'as if' technique.
– WILLIAM JAMES, US PSYCHOLOGIST, DOCTOR AND PHILOSOPHER

In other words, fake it till you make it! Basically when it comes to personality traits, there is no difference between possessing them and pretending to have them. Remember Carl Simonton from Chapter 43 (page 95), who said that, 'mind, body and emotions are a unitary system – affect one and you affect the others'. This means that you can pretend to be confident or courageous and the cocktail of chemicals inside your body for those attributes will be created and you will indeed feel confidence or courageous. Pretending you have a character trait such as confidence is not the same as pretending you can scale mountains or play the tuba. Those particular skills must be learned. Characteristics such as courage, confidence and enthusiasm are created in the mind by the pictures you create, though.

Acting as if sets a positive expectation. Remember the definition of self-fulfilling prophecy from Chapter 26 (page 61). We believe something to be true and then act in a way that brings that assumption about. This can be a positive or negative force.

The effect of self-fulfilling prophecies has been demonstrated by objective scientific experiments. In one study at the start of the 1968 school year, Dr R. Rosenthal gave a non-verbal intelligence test to 18 classrooms of elementary school students in a Californian public school district. Twenty per cent of the students selected randomly, not on test score, were then identified as 'intellectual bloomers' and their teachers were told they could expect to see remarkable intellectual gains in the coming year. The only difference between these students and the other 80% was the expectations created in the teachers' minds. When both groups were retested, 8 months later, the 'bloomers' had gained in IQ points over the other group. This is significant because it shows that altered expectations can result in unconscious changes in behaviour that dramatically change the outcome.

In another study during the 1970s, 152 cancer patients were assessed based on their expectation and attitude about their treatment and then each was monitored for 18 months. The results clearly indicated those with a positive expectation about the treatment got the best results. It follows therefore that your chances of success in anything in life are greatly improved by positive expectations.

Collier quotes from *Applied Psychology and Scientific Living*, where author David Bush states, 'Man is like the wireless operator. Man is subject to miscellaneous wrong through currents if his mind is not in tune with the Infinite, or if he is not keyed up to higher vibrations than those of negation'.

HERE'S AN IDEA FOR YOU...

If there are traits that you don't possess and you would like to have them, look for someone who has those traits in real life and read their biography. Now take on their persona when you need it. Ask yourself, what would X do?

47 SPECIALIST VS GENERALIST

Collier tells how despite being a comparatively small part of the services assisting during World War I, the Salvation Army got the lion's share of the glory. He asks, *'Do you know how they did it? By concentrating on just one thing – DOUGHNUTS!'*

DEFINING IDEA...

The aim of marketing is to know and understand the customer so well the product or service fits him and sells itself.

~ PETER F. DRUCKER, MANAGEMENT CONSULTANT AND WRITER

In 1917, Helen Purviance – an ensign in the Salvation Army – was sent to France to work with the American First Division. She and her fellow officer, Ensign Margaret Sheldon, decided to make doughnuts for the troops. Using a wine bottle to roll out the dough and cut a hole in the middle of each one, they were able to fry 7 at a time in an army helmet, making 150 doughnuts that first day. They were a huge success and soon hundreds of women along the frontline trenches were making up to 9,000 doughnuts a day! Soldiers cheered the 'doughnut girls' as the simple little treat eased the hardship of frontline fighting.

According to Collier, this dedication to doing one thing really well is the hallmark of success in any endeavour, including business. Although the Salvation Army did more than make doughnuts all day long, it is what they are best remembered for.

You might argue that Henry Ford, regarded by many as the father of mass production, followed this principle to the letter, but it didn't pan out too well for him. By 1920, one Model T every minute rolled off the production line. Ford was doing one thing, and doing it very well, but what he didn't appreciate was that as soon as people got used to the idea that they could own a car, they didn't all want to own the same car! Over at General Motors, however, Alfred P. Sloan believed his company could still do one thing very well – make cars. But in a marketing first, Sloan split the market into more detailed segments, targeting each of his five models – Chevrolet, Oldsmobile, Pontiac, Buick and Cadillac – to a particular demographic of the car-buying market.

The idea that you should focus your business on one key product or service rings as true today as it was when the Salvation Army were dishing out doughnuts. Now the only difference is that you must pitch that one product or service in a slightly different way to different audiences.

You can see this with any tour operator. They don't say, 'Book your holiday with us.' That's just weak and meaningless. Instead, brochures are targeted to particular niche groups within the holiday-buying population – honeymoons, family friendly, cruise, adventures, and so on. The basic product and service they offer is the same, but it's packaged up to resonate directly with target groups within the mass market.

Collier encourages us to concentrate all our energies on a single idea and 'apply that same principle to the building of a business'.

HERE'S AN IDEA FOR YOU...

If you are in business, forget marketing to large market segments. Instead, break them down into niche groups and tailor your message to each target group. Mass marketing won't work, so don't waste your money.

48 INITIATIVE

Collier talks of the big manhunt of industry and how those at the top, *'always have a weather eye open for the promising material. And the thing they value most of all is initiative.'* Here is another invisible human quality that often translates into wealth.

DEFINING IDEA...
Change yourself; change your fortunes.
~ PORTUGUESE PROVERB

Collier states, 'The trouble with most men is that they think they have done all that is required of them when they have earned their salary.' Somewhere along the line the employer/employee relationship became combative, rather than cooperative. As a result, millions do the bare minimum in exchange for their pay. But this approach doesn't work. Not only does it deprive workers of the opportunity to make more money, more importantly, it deprives them of the opportunity to feel a sense of personal fulfilment, pride and satisfaction from a job well done.

Sooner or later we all have to take responsibility for the situations we find ourselves in. If we don't like our job, we must take responsibility for that and accept or change it. Bitching about it won't help anyone. When we can see how we create our own bed prior to lying in it, we can tap into greater resources and find the initiative to make the necessary changes.

Remember Aren Ralston from Chapter 42 (page 92). In an interview with *National Geographic*, he was asked how he finally decided to cut off his own arm. He said, 'After having enough sleep deprived, meandering thoughts about how I arrived in the canyon, I realized that my situation was the result of decisions that I had made. I chose to go out there by myself. I chose to not tell anyone where I was going. I chose not to go with two climbers I had met in the canyon on the first day. But I also realized that I had made all of the choices up to that point that had helped me survive. I took responsibility for all of my decisions, which helped me take on the responsibility of getting myself out.'

And if Ralston can take responsibility for making some poor choices that almost killed him and find the strength and initiative to do what needed to be done to change his situation, surely the rest of us can find the strength and determination to change the things in our lives that make us unhappy. Thankfully we may never need to amputate our own arm, but we must all take responsibility for our own well-being and happiness. No knight, shining or otherwise, is going to appear on a white horse to save you!

Collier says, 'Remember, you must give to get and it is when you give that extra bit of time and attention and thought to your work that you begin to stand out above the crowd around you'.

HERE'S AN IDEA FOR YOU...

When there is something in your life that you don't like, you have to change it! If you hate your job, either do it better than you've ever done it before so you get promoted to a more suitable role or leave and find something that you can throw your heart and soul into.

49 PRICELESS WISDOM OF BOOKS

Collier says, *'There is priceless wisdom to be found in books. As Carlyle put it – All that mankind has done, thought, gained or been, is lying in matchless preservation in the pages of books.'* Sadly, harbingers of doom have been talking about the end of the humble book for years.

You can now read books in the old-fashioned way or on your laptop computer, or even on your son's Nintendo DS, if you so wish. There are various electronic readers such as the Sony Reader and the Kindle, but you still can't beat a book.

People talk of physical books as though they are not long for this world. And while I may be biased, I can't imagine a world without books. In fact, far from making them obsolete, advances in technology are bringing some back to life.

DEFINING IDEA...
There are worse crimes than burning books. One of them is not reading them.
~ JOSEPH BRODSKY, POET

In July 2009, Amazon teamed up with the University of Michigan to print 400,000 rare, out-of-print and out-of-copyright titles from its library, including an 1898 book by Florence Nightingale called *Notes on Nursing: What It is and What It Is Not*. This has been made possible by the university's project to digitise its collection in partnership with Google, who aim to put every book ever written online. University of Michigan libraries Dean Paul Courant said the arrangement means, 'books unavailable for a century or more will be able to go back into print, one copy at a time'.

Of course, there are challenges with all these innovations, not least how to pay the authors, but if these issues can be resolved fairly then the idea of having every book ever written available to buy in book form or to view online is phenomenal.

Writing a book is a considerable undertaking and according to bookstatistics. com, it takes 475 hours to write the average fiction title and 725 hours to write a work of non-fiction. A book is considered successful if it sells 5,000 (fiction) and 7,500 (non-fiction). And in case you might be wondering, people do indeed judge a book by its cover. According to a survey by the *Wall Street Journal*, a bookstore browser spends 8 seconds looking at the front cover and 15 seconds studying the back cover.

Whether from a physical book, eBook or online websites, our access to information and knowledge is at an all-time high. True, some of it is utter nonsense, but you are now only clicks away from knowing how to bake the perfect Pavlova, build a straw bale house or toilet train your pooch.

So, get reading! 'The truths which mankind has been laboriously learning through countless ages, at who knows what price of sweat and toil and starvation and blood – all are yours for the effort of reading them.' There are some lessons that you don't have to do for yourself – learn from others through books and save time, energy, even tears.

HERE'S AN IDEA FOR YOU...

You know that book you bought recently? Read it! According to Bookstatistics. com, most people don't get past page 18 of the books they purchase. If that statistic resonates with you, pick up one of the books from your reading pile and get started, now!

50 AGE IS IRRELEVANT

Collier states, *'Youth is not a matter of time. It is a mental state. The whole purpose of existence is Growth. Life is dynamic – not static. It is ever moving forward – not standing still.'* Indeed, when we stop growing, we stagnate and die. Years don't matter, but using your brain does!

If you were to visit the School Sisters of Notre Dame nunnery in remote Mankato, Minnesota, you would find that many of the sisters are older than ninety. Sister Marcella Zachman didn't stop teaching until she was ninety-seven, while Sister Mary Esther Boor worked the front desk until she was ninety-nine! Both featured in a 1994 story in *Life* magazine.

> DEFINING IDEA...
> *Forty is the old age of youth; fifty is the youth of old age.*
> ~ VICTOR HUGO, FRENCH WRITER AND STATESMAN

David Snowdon of the University of Kentucky has been studying these nuns to find clues as to why they age so well and have fewer and milder cases of dementia, Alzheimer's and other brain diseases. The nuns believe that 'an idle mind is the Devil's plaything' and as such, constantly challenge themselves with vocabulary quizzes, puzzles and lively debate. Upon their death, over 100 of the nuns donated their brains to further Snowdon's investigation, in which he discovered that the axons and dendrites that usually shrink with age instead branched out and so made new connections in these brains. His conclusion was that intellectually challenging activities stimulate dendritic growth and increase neural connections. If the brain is then damaged by a stroke or disease, it can reroute messages and limit the debilitating effects.

At the other end of the spectrum, I read a very interesting story about the entrepreneur Richard Branson. Apparently while on a drive with his mother Eve – miles from their home – Eve asked Richard (four years old at the time) if he thought he could find his way home from where he was. Although he was completely unfamiliar with the area, the miniature Branson thought he could and so his mother stopped the car and he hopped out. Apparently Eve Branson was determined to make her children independent. By twelve, Branson was making 100-mile round trips to Bournemouth alone on his bike. Undoubtedly, his mother's brave and courageous choices in how she raised her son created the resourceful man he is today. And yes, he found his way home!

Incidentally, twelve is the same age as US First Admiral David Farragut when he took command of a captured British ship off the coast of Peru and sailed it to Boston. It's also the same age as George Washington when he dropped out of school and Thomas Jefferson when he began managing 250 employees on a large plantation in Virginia.

Perhaps limiting ourselves by expectation based on nothing more than a number is foolish, after all. Collier says, 'It is for men and women who are not ready to stand still, who refuse to cease to grow, that [*The Secret of the Ages*] is written.'

HERE'S AN IDEA FOR YOU...

Collier makes a very valid assessment when he says there is only one difference between youth and age: 'Youth looks forward always to something better. Age looks backwards and sighs over its "lost" youth.' Stop looking back and get excited about your future, whatever age you are!

51 THE MEDICINAL DELUSION

Apparently US physician and author, Professor Oliver Wendell Holmes, said, 'If 99% of all the drugs we possess were thrown into the sea it would be a good thing for the human race, but rather hard on the fishes.' Collier states, *'The day of the Indian Medicine Man and street-corner fakir has passed.'* Sadly, he was wrong.

Now the only difference in the 'street-corner fakir' is billion dollar pharmaceutical monsters. Illness, real and imagined, is big money. And the question has to be asked: is the drug industry seeking to find cures for disease, or are they simply happy to line their pockets treating the symptoms?

DEFINING IDEA...

Doctors are men who prescribe medicines of which they know little, to cure disease of which they know less, in human beings of whom they know nothing.

~ VOLTAIRE, FRENCH WRITER AND ESSAYIST

In a report by the US Department of Health and Human Services half of severely depressed patients taking drugs improved versus 32% taking a placebo. Considering the antidepressant industry is worth $8.2 billion alone, surely patients might expect a better result than that? In 'The Emperor's New Drugs', an article published in the American Psychological Association's *Prevention & Treatment*, in 2002 University of Connecticut psychology professor Irving Kirsch found that 80% of the effect of antidepressants, as measured in clinical trials, could be attributed to the placebo effect. Kirsch actually had to invoke the *Freedom of Information Act* in 2001 to gain access to the data. In a Discovery Health Channel interview, Kirsch said, 'The difference between the response of the drugs and the response of placebo was less than two points on average on this clinical scale that goes from fifty to sixty points. That's a very small difference. That difference clinically is meaningless.'

So, the results of antidepressants for the drug companies making them is billions of dollars in profit, while the results for most of those patients taking them could, in truth, be matched by taking a Smartie! Provided, of course, the sweet was prescribed by a trusted doctor and they believed it was going to help them.

What is amazing about these stories is not that the drugs really don't work, but that placebos do. Indeed, it's so amazing that you might think the placebo effect would be the subject of major, well-funded research. After all, if we could understand how belief in the curative properties of a 'drug' bring about the expected cure, even when there are no pharmaceutical properties, then medicine would have an inexpensive method for treating a whole host of diseases and disorders, with no side effects either.

And it is true that the drug companies are indeed studying the placebo effect, but not so that they can share those results with the wider community. Their studies allow them to effectively eliminate those susceptible to the placebo effect from their clinical trials and therefore improve statistics!

Collier reminds us, 'Mind is the Healer. Drugs can sometimes make its work easier by removing obstructions, by killing off parasites. But the regular use of drugs is far more likely to harm than to heal.'

HERE'S AN IDEA FOR YOU...

My step-kids have recently got it into their heads that they get car sick, despite the fact that they travelled happily for years. We now give them a vitamin pill, but tell them it's a travel sickness pill and it works a treat. Try it!

52 AND FINALLY... THE MINDBENDER

'I can believe all you say about my fears and worries being responsible for my "own illnesses", write many people, "but how about infants and little children? They have no fear. Why do they sicken and die?"' Collier suggests this is because the subconscious is susceptible to the suggestion of others.

DEFINING IDEA...
How people treat you is their karma; how you react is yours.
~ WAYNE DYER, AUTHOR

But there is a more controversial explanation – reincarnation. The concept of karma and reincarnation is a cornerstone of many religions, including Hinduism, Buddhism, Taoism and Kabbala (as ascribed to by Madonna). It is also found in cultures as wide ranging as African tribes, American Indians, Polynesian Kahunas and the Druids.

In the 1980s, psychiatry professor Dr Joel Whitton researched what we unconsciously know about ourselves under hypnosis and his evidence strongly suggests the reality of reincarnation. Patients regressed to the space between lives told of planning their next life, including the major significant events that they would experience. But this was not some fairy-tale wish list waiting room. One woman, who had been raped when she was thirty-seven, realised that she had actually planned the event before she entered her current life because it had been necessary to force her to change her 'entire soul complexion'. Another client realised he'd chosen a serious kidney disease as punishment for a past life transgression.

In other words, that karmic justice I mentioned in Chapter 32 (page 72) doesn't begin and end in one lifetime – the debts are on-going and sooner or later in this lifetime or the next, we will all be called to account. And that is why children get sick and bad things happen to good people. We only see one incarnation, but there are many lives before to account for. It's not all negative, though, we also have karmic bonds to certain souls, who we will live out many lifetimes, in differing relationships.

If you find all this a little hard to take in, you are not alone. Florida psychiatrist Brian Weiss, a graduate of Yale Medical School, was extremely sceptical about reincarnation until under hypnosis, one of his patients started to talk spontaneously about her past lives, many of which he was able to verify. He wrote up his extraordinary findings in his book, *Many Lives, Many Masters*, published in 1988.

Stanislav Grof, another psychiatrist who has worked extensively in this area, says: 'The opening of the realm of past incarnation experiences is sometimes associated with complex insights and instructions. In this way, the individual is introduced to the understanding that the Law of Karma is an important part of cosmic order.' And in case you're wondering, many of those subjects who experienced past-life memories were adamant it was all complete nonsense.

Regardless of what you make of this, remember the truth in Collier's words for this lifetime, 'Babies and young children fall such easy victims to the fears of disease and contagion of their parents and those around them.'

HERE'S AN IDEA FOR YOU...

If someone could prove categorically that reincarnation and karma was real – and therefore that you would have to experience every bad thing you ever did, whether you were caught doing it or not – would you live your life differently?

CONCLUSION

The Secret of the Ages is a fantastic little book. It is full of classic lines that I have seen repeated countless times by others (although rarely attributed to Collier). However, his message is not unique and has been told in various forms for generations. What makes the book special, though, is Collier's use of metaphor and analogy to make his point. He had a way with words that captures the imagination and gives his writing depth.

Writing in this manner can be a powerful way to help readers gain a quick and almost holographic understanding of new concepts, something Collier did brilliantly. One of my favourites is when he is describing the human condition and likens it to a turtle stuck on his back! *'For a while it threshes around wildly, reaching for something outside to take hold of that shall put it on its feet. Just as we humans always look for help outside ourselves first, but presently he draws all his forces within his shell, rests a bit to regain his strength, and then throws his whole force to one side – legs, head, tail and all – and over he goes!'*

How true is that! Collier suggests we all stop threshing about, trying in vain to grab onto external solutions, excuses or justifications for the predicaments we find ourselves in. Instead, we should go inside and learn how to tap into the power of our own mind.

I first became aware of many of the ideas presented in Collier's *The Secret of the Ages* when I was in my early teens. Today, as I finish this book, I am thirty-nine years old. For most of those years, I have been fascinated by the capability of the human mind. I have read ferociously on the subject, attended countless courses and seminars – some of them on the fringes of accepted sanity! Collier writes of the power of thought to shape our lives and how so few of us truly appreciate just how potent a force this is.

I know this to be true. For me, it is one of the fundamental truths of life. And yet despite everything, occasionally I still forget, I still get bogged down with the day-to-day of life. Sometimes I would rather wallow a little longer in my self-pity and irritation, but then a little voice quietly nudges me and reminds me that I could just change my mind, but I confess there are days when I ignore it! After all, blaming others can be so emotionally rewarding. The problem is that once you've read books like *The Secret of the Ages* and experienced their truth for yourself, you can't un-know it! It's like opening Pandora's box – blame and recrimination become foolish and pointless. Instead, you finally appreciate that you are the only one who can change things.

The great news is that there really is an extremely simple way to change and that is to change your thoughts, but like so many simple things it's not always that easy. This is not a one-time revelation. I have absolute faith in the power of the mind in the same way that I know the sun will rise tomorrow, yet I still have to remind myself to choose a different thought. Sometimes I have to drag myself kicking and screaming from my old thought into a new one, but when I do so, it works. Remember, as the poet John Milton once said, 'The mind is its own place, and in itself can make heaven of hell, a hell of heaven.'

REFERENCE MATERIAL

IDEA 1
A Short History of Nearly Everything by Bill Bryson, pp. 29, 543
The God Delusion by Richard Dawkins, pp. 242, 243

IDEA 2
The Ten Best Mothers of All Time by Sean Cunningham, *Esquire Magazine*, 8 May 2009
Some Factors Modifying the Expression of Human Strength by Michio Ikai and Arthur H. Steinhaus, *Journal of Applied Physiology*, pp. 157–163, 1961

IDEA 3
What the Bleep Do we Know: Discovering the Endless Possibilities for Altering Your Everyday Reality by William Arntz, Betsy Chasse and Mark Vicente, p.14
A Short History of Nearly Everything by Bill Bryson, p. 223

IDEA 4
The Subconscious Mind: Your Unsung Hero by Kate Douglas, *New Scientist Magazine*, issue 2632, 1 December 2007
The Biology of Belief: Unleashing the Power of Consciousness, Matter & Miracles by Bruce H. Lipton Ph.D., p. 97
A User's Guide to the Brain by John Ratey, p. 10

IDEA 5
Blink: The Power of Thinking Without Thinking by Malcolm Gladwell, pp. 3–6, 23

IDEA 6
The Holographic Universe by Michael Talbot, p. 142

IDEA 7
The Holographic Universe by Michael Talbot, pp. 60–1
Unlimited Power by Anthony Robbins, p. 183

IDEA 8
Temple Grandin, official website
Savant for a Day by Lawrence Osborne, *The New York Times*, 22 June 2003

IDEA 9
Quantum Healing: Exploring the Frontiers of Mind/Body Medicine by Deepak Chopra M.D., p. 155

Patient-controlled Analgesia and Intra-operative Suggestion by P. Dawson, C. Van Hamel, D. Wilkinson, P. Warwick and M. O'Connor, *Anaesthesia Magazine*, 1 February 2001

Intra-operative Therapeutic Suggestion in Day-case Surgery: Are There Benefits for Post-operative Outcome? by A. H. Lebovits, R. Twersky and B. McEwan, *British Journal of Anaesthesia*, p. 82, 1999

Epinephrine Enables Pavlovian Fear Conditioning Under Anesthesia by N. M. Weinberger, P. E. Gold and D. B. Sternberg, *Science*, 10 February 1984

IDEA 10
Conscious Acts of Creation: The Emergence of a New Physics by William A. Tiller Ph.D., Walter E. Dibble Jr Ph.D. and Michael J. Kohane Ph.D. p. 392

What the Bleep Do We Know: Discovering the Endless Possibilities for Altering Your Everyday Reality by William Arntz, Betsy Chasse and Mark Vicente, p. 29

IDEA 11
The Biology of Belief: Unleashing the Power of Consciousness, Matter & Miracles by Bruce H. Lipton Ph.D., pp. 94, 112

IDEA 12
What the Bleep Do We Know: Discovering the Endless Possibilities for Altering Your Everyday Reality by William Arntz, Betsy Chasse and Mark Vicente, pp. 53, 56, 110

IDEA 15
A User's Guide to the Brain by John Ratey, pp. 24, 31, 59

Journal of Neurophysiology, vol. 74, issue 3, 1995

Modulation of Muscle Responses Evoked By Transcranial Magnetic Stimulation During the Acquisition of New Fine Motor Skills by A. Pascual-Leone, D. Nguyet, L. G. Cohen, J. P. Brasil-Neto, A. Cammarota and M. Hallett

IDEA 16
The Theory of Moral Sentiments by Adam Smith, Professor of Moral Philosophy in the University of Glasgow, 1759

Weapons of Mass Instruction: A Schoolteacher's Journey through the Dark World of Compulsory Schooling by John Taylor Gatto, p. 52

IDEA 18
Peak Performance: Mental Training Techniques of the World's Greatest Athletes by Charles A. Garfield, Ph.D., with Hal Zina Bennett, p. 16

IDEA 19
The Tipping Point: How Little Things Can Make a Big Difference by Malcolm Gladwell, pp. 5, 141, 142

Freakonomics: A Rogue Economist Explores the Hidden Side of Everything by Steven D. Levitt and Stephen J. Dubner, pp. 3, 4

IDEA 20
The Biology of Belief: Unleashing the Power of Consciousness, Matter & Miracles by Bruce H. Lipton Ph.D., pp. xv, 42, 96

IDEA 21
The (Real!) Science Behind Lie to Me by S. E. Kramer, *Popular Mechanics Magazine*, 21 January 2009

IDEA 22
Everyday Enlightenment: The Twelve Gateways to Personal Growth by Dan Millman, p. 153

IDEA 23
Evolve Your Brain: The Science of Changing Your Mind by Joe Dispenza D.C., pp. 49, 184

IDEA 24
Credit Action: Better Thinking About Money: Debt Facts and Figures, compiled 1 August 2009

IDEA 25
Blink: The Power of Thinking Without Thinking by Malcolm Gladwell, pp. 20, 21, 32, 33

IDEA 28
Research Affirms Power of Positive Thinking by Daniel Goleman, *The New York Times*, 3 February 1987

IDEA 29
BBC 3 Freaky Eaters website

IDEA 30
Yes! 50 Secrets from the Science of Persuasion by Noah J. Goldstein Ph.D., Steve J. Martin and Robert B. Cialdini Ph.D., pp. 38, 39

IDEA 31
Sacred Contracts: Awakening Your Divine Potential by Caroline Myss, p. 19
Natural Born Success: Discover the Instinctive Drives That Make You Tick by Paul Burgess

IDEA 32
What the Bleep Do We Know: Discovering the Endless Possibilities for Altering Your Everyday Reality by William Arntz, Betsy Chasse and Mark Vicente, pp. 203, 269
The Seven Spiritual Laws of Success: A Practical Guide to the Fulfilment of Your Dreams by Deepak Chopra, pp. 35, 45

IDEA 34
How to be Rich Working Two Days a Week by Brendan Nichols, p. 145
Living in the Light: A Guide to Personal and Planetary Transformation by Shakti Gawain, p. 25

IDEA 35
The Ascent of Money A Financial History of the World by Niall Ferguson, p. 237
Credit Action: Debt Facts and Figures, complied 1 August 2009

IDEA 36
Quantum Healing: Exploring the Frontiers of Mind/Body Medicine by Deepak Chopra M.D., p. 44
The Holographic Universe by Michael Talbot, p. 150

IDEA 37
What the Bleep Do We Know: Discovering the Endless Possibilities for Altering Your Everyday Reality by William Arntz, Betsy Chasse and Mark Vicente, p. 15
Getting Well Again by O. Carl Simonton, Stephanie Matthews-Simonton and James L. Creighton, pp. 56–9
Sacred Contracts: Awakening Your Divine Potential by Caroline Myss, p. 19

IDEA 38
The God Delusion by Richard Dawkins, p. 58

IDEA 39
What the Bleep Do We Know: Discovering the Endless Possibilities for Altering Your Everyday Reality by William Arntz, Betsy Chasse and Mark Vicente, p. 164

IDEA 40
Research Affirms Power of Positive Thinking by Daniel Goleman, *The New York Times*, 3 February 1987

IDEA 42
Climber Who Cut Off Hand Looks Back by Michael Benoist, *National Geographic Adventure*, 30 August 2004
Touching the Void, *Wikipedia*

IDEA 43
Getting Well Again by O. Carl Simonton, Stephanie Matthews-Simonton and James L. Creighton, p. 31
What the Bleep Do We Know: Discovering the Endless Possibilities for Altering Your Everyday Reality by William Arntz, Betsy Chasse and Mark Vicente, p. 160
The Heart's Code: Tapping the Wisdom and Power of Our Heart Energy by Paul Pearsall Ph.D., p. 42

IDEA 45
Blink: The Power of Thinking Without Thinking by Malcolm Gladwell, p. 51
Touching the Void, *Wikipedia*

IDEA 46
Getting Well Again by O. Carl Simonton, Stephanie Matthews-Simonton and James L. Creighton, pp. 81, 82

IDEA 47
Doughnut: the Official Story, Worldwar1.com website
The 75 Greatest Management Decisions Ever Made… And Some of the Worst by Stuart Crainer, p. 49

IDEA 48
Climber Who Cut Off Hand Looks Back by Michael Benoist, *National Geographic Adventure*, 30 August 2004

IDEA 49
University of Michigan Expands Print on Demand Effort with Amazon's Booksurge, *Publishers Weekly Magazine*, 22 July 2009

IDEA 50
Weapons of Mass Instruction: A Schoolteacher's Journey Through the Dark World of Compulsory Schooling by John Taylor Gatto, pp. 29, 33
A User's Guide to the Brain by John Ratey, pp. 42, 43

IDEA 51
The Biology of Belief: Unleashing the Power of Consciousness, Matter & Miracles by Bruce H. Lipton Ph.D., pp. 107, 108

IDEA 52
Holographic Universe by Michael Talbot, pp. 216, 295
The Adventure of Self-Discovery: Dimensions of Consciousness and New Perspectives in Psychotherapy and Inner Exploration by Stanislav Grof, pp. 86–7

INDEX

Note: page numbers in bold indicate *Defining ideas* or *Here's an idea for you* sections.

A

ageing, 108–9
associative learning, 54–5
attitude, 30–1
    acting as if, 100–1
    optimism, 64–5
autism, 24–5, 48

B

belief, 10–11, 30–1, 100–1
    placebo effect, 110–11
Bernard, Claude, 48–9
The Bible, 84
biofeedback, 95
body *see* medical events
Bohm, David, 23
books, 106–7
Branson, Richard, 109
'broken window' theory, 47
Brownsville, New York, 46–7
Bruno, Giordano, 14–15
Bryson, Bill, 10
Burgess, Paul, 71
Bush, David, *Applied Psychology and Scientific Living*, 101
Business Impact of Writing a Book, The, 63
business *see* working life

C

Carlyle, Thomas, 106
Carnegie, Andrew, 40
Cavallo, Angela and Tony, 12
change, 76–7, 77, 87, **105**, 115
    acting as if, 100–1
    procrastination and, 96–7
children, **61**, 112–13

Chopra, Deepak, *Quantum Healing*, 80
collective consciousness, 22–3, 33, 98–9
    as Universal Mind, 17, 22, 60–1, 77, 95, 99
    prayer, 28–9
    see also subconscious and conscious mind; thought
Collier, Robert, 36
    Secret of the Ages, 8–9, 114–15
conscious mind *see* subconscious and conscious mind
Copernicus, Nicolas, 14
Creationism, 10
Credit Action, 56
credit crunch, 56–7, 78–9
criminology, 46–7, 51

D

Dawkins, Richard, 11
Dayan, Peter, 16
debt, 56–7, 78–9
Dehaene, Stanislas, 16
depression, 83, **83**, **85**, 110–11
Descarte, Rene, 82
discouragement, 74–5
Dostoevsky, Fyodor, 34
drug companies, 110–11

E

education, 41
    and learning, 54–5, 64–5
Einstein, Albert, 23
Ekman, Dr Paul, 50
Ellis, Albert, 82
emotion, 94–5
emulation, **101**
Epigenics, 49
evolution of knowledge, 14–15
    neurological research, 16
evolution of the world, 10, 15

F

facial expressions, 50–1, 59
fear, 14, 78–9, 84–5
    accepting, 86–7
Feynman, Richard, 32–3
fire walking, 81, **81**
Fischer, Bobby, 69
food fetishes, 66–7

Ford, Henry, 102–3
Freakonomics, 47
Freaky Eaters (tv show), 66–7
Freud, Sigmund, 16
Friedman, Dr Meyer, Type A Behaviour and Your Heart, 83

G

Galen, 83
Galileo Galilei, 15
Gandhi, Mohandas, 76
Garfield, Charles, *Peak Performance*, 44–5
Gatto, John Taylor, 41
genetics, 49
germ theory, 48
Getty Museum, 18–19
Gladwell, Malcolm
    Blink, 18
    The Tipping Point, 46
goal setting, 60–1, 100–1
Gottman, John, 58–9
Grandin, Temple, 24–5
Green, Elmer and Alyce, 95
Grof, Stanislav, 113

H

Haraldsson, Erlendur, 81
health *see* medical events
Hebbian learning, 54–5
Hill, Napoleon, *Think and Grow Rich*, 8, 12, **95**
Hillman, James, **97**
Holmes, Professor Oliver Wendell, 110
Hooke, Robert, 9
How to Write a Book in 33 Days, 63
hypnosis, 30–1

I

ID (Instinctive Drives) System, 71, **71**
Ikai, Michio, 12–13
information, 106–7
initiative, 104–5
innate talents, 40–1, 70–1
insomnia, 53, 90
intuition, 18–19

J

J. Paul Getty Museum, 18–19
Jacobsen, Edmund, 90
Jahn, Robert, 20
James, William, 9, 31
John of Salisbury, 'Metalogicon,' 8
Journal of Applied Psychology, 13
Jung, Carl, 22

K

karmic justice, 72–3, 112–13, **113**
Kelling, George, 47
Kirsh, Irving, 110–11

L

learning, 54–5, 64–5
Ledwith, Dr Miceal, 32, 72
Lie to Me (tv show), 50
Life Principle (superhuman abilities), 12–13, 92–3
Lipton, Bruce H., *The Biology of Belief*, 17, 26, 31
Loeb, Jacques, 92
Londe, Sam, 31

M

MacLean, Paul, 16
marketing, 102–3, **103**
marriage, 58–9
    and parenthood, **61**, 74, **75**, 97, **111**, 113
Mason, Dr Albert, 30
Meador, Clifton, 31
media, influence of, 36–7
medical events
    belief and, 30–1
        placebo effect, 110–11
    children, 111–13
    fear and, 84–5
    mind and body, 82–3
        mind over matter, 80–1
        relaxation, 90–1
    post-operative healing, 26–7
meditation, 52–3, **53**
mental rehearsal, 44–5
Merton, Robert K., *Social Theory and Social Structure*, 61
micro expressions, 50–1
Millman, Dan, *Everyday Enlightenment*, 53

mind and body, 82–3
mind over matter, 80–1
relaxation, 90–1
Myss, Caroline, 83
Sacred Contracts, 70

N

Naisbitt, John, 19
Neural Darwinism, 38
neuroscience, 16–17, 38–9, 54–5
see also thought
New Thought movement, 9, 28
New York University Medical Center, 27
Newton, Isaac, 8–9
Nichols, Brendan, 76
Nightingale, Florence, 106
Notre Dame nunnery, Minnesota, 108

O

open-mindedness, 14–15
optimism, 64–5, 88–9

P

Paget, Sir James, 'Surgical Pathology,' 83
parenthood, 61, 74, 75, 97, 111, 113
Pavlovian procedures, 13
perception, 62–3
pessimism, 31
physics *see* quantum physics
Pitzer, Dr., 10
placebo effect, 110–11
prayer, 28–9
procrastination, 96
Progressive Muscle Relaxation (PMR), 90–1
psychiatry, 112–13
psychology, 9, 35, 44–5, 64–5
hypnosis, 30–1
Purviance, Helen, 102
Puthoff, Harold, 10
Pygmalion Effect, 85

Q

quantum physics, 23, 32–3, 33

R

Ralston, Aren, 92–3, 104–5
reality, 32, 86–7
reciprocity, 68–9, 72–3
relaxation, 90–1
religion, 84–5
fundamentalism, 10–11, 14–15
reincarnation, 112–13
remote viewing, 20–1
responsibility, 104–5
Romen, Alexander, 44
Roseman, Ray, *Type A Behaviour and Your Heart*, 83
Rosenthal, Dr R, 101

S

Sai Baba, Sathya, 81
Salvation Army, 102–3
savants, 24–5
self-awareness, 42–3, 76–7, 114
change, 76–7, 77
facial expressions, 50–1, 59
innate talents, 40–1, 70–1
presumed truths, 48–9
self-fulfilling prophecy, 61, 100–1
Seligman, Dr Martin, 64, 65, 88
Sheldon, Margaret, 102
Silva method, 21
Simonton, Dr Carl, 82, 83, 95, 100
Simpson, Joe, 93, 98–9
sleep, 53, 88, 90
Sloan, Alfred P., 103
Smith, Adam, *The Theory of Moral Sentiments*, 40
Snowdon, David, 108
Snyder, Dr Allan, 25
Soros, George, 99
sporting performance, 44
Steinhaus, Arthur H., 12–13
Stevenson, Robert Louis, 42
stress management, 90–1
subconscious and conscious mind, 16–17
emotion, 94–5
intuition, 18–19
post-operative healing and, 26–7
remote viewing, 20–1
savants and, 24–5
self-awareness, 42–3
presumed truths, 48–9
susceptibility to the suggestion of

others, 112–14
  see also collective consciousness; thought
superhuman abilities, 12–13, 92–3
superstitions, 48–9
survival stories, 92–3

T

Talbot, Michael, *The Holographic Universe*, 81
Targ, Russell, 20
Taylor, Frank Bursley, 15
The Secret of the Ages, 8–9
thin-slicing, 19
thought
  intelligence and choice, 40–1, 115
    associative learning, 54–5, **55**
  mind over matter, 80–1
  negative and positive, 34–5, 51, 64–5
    age and, 88–9
    media influences and, 36–7
    meditation and, 52–3, **53**
    self-fulfilling prophecy, 61, 100–1
  visualisation, 44–5, 60–1
  see also collective consciousness;
neuroscience; subconscious and conscious mind
Tiller, William, *Conscious Acts of Creation*, 28–9, 33
tolerance, 10–11

U

Universal Mind, 17, 22, 60–1, 77, 95, 99
  as collective consciousness, 22–3, 33, 98–9
University of Western Australia, 35

V

Vidal, Gore, 85
virtue, 100–1
visualisation, 44–5, 60–1, 67

W

Walshe, Walter Hyle, 83
Watson, Lyall, 22–3
Weinberger, Sterberg and Gold (1984), 27
Weiss, Brian, *Many Lives, Many Masters*, 113
Western Australia, University of, 35
What the Bleep Do We Know!?, **33**
Whitton, Dr Joel, 112
Wilson, James, 47
working life, 56–7, **57**
  image and perception, 62–3
  initiative, 104–5
  marketing, 102–3, **103**

Y

Yates, Simon, 93, 98–9

Made in the USA
Middletown, DE
28 August 2022